GEORGE WASHINGTON'S SECRET SIX

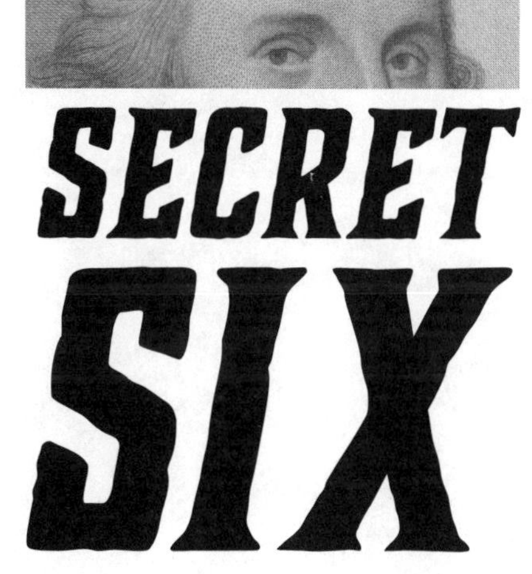

GEORGE WASHINGTON'S SECRET SIX

The Spies Who Saved America

Brian Kilmeade & Don Yaeger

VIKING

VIKING
An imprint of Penguin Random House LLC, New York

First published in the United States of America by Viking,
an imprint of Penguin Random House LLC, 2019

LIBRARY OF CONGRESS CATALOGING-IN-PUBLICATION DATA IS AVAILABLE.
ISBN 9780425288986

Printed in USA

10 9 8 7 6 5 4 3 2 1

To all of America's history teachers, especially my eighth grade social studies instructor, Mr. Don Nobile. Mr Nobile's storytelling ignited my passion for our nation's history, specifically that of our presidents, which still burns today.

–BK

To Will and Madeleine: May a passion for our nation's history always inspire you to read, learn and change the world. I love you both!

—DY

Washington did not really outfight the British, he simply outspied us!

Major George Beckwith,
British intelligence officer, 1782–83

The great objects of information you are very well acquainted with: such as Arrivals, Embarkations, Preparations for Movements, alteration of Positions, situation of Posts, Fortifications, Garrisons, strength or weakness of each, distribution and strength of Corps, and in general every thing which can be interesting and important for us to know. Besides these, you are also sensible there are many things upon a smaller scale, which are necessary to be reported: and that whatever intelligence is communicated, ought to be, not in general terms, but in detail, and with the greatest precision.

General George Washington,
in a letter to Benjamin Tallmadge, April 1781

Contents

PART THREE

PART FOUR

Appendixes

A Note from the Author

Dear Reader,

There are many reasons why I am flat-out thrilled to share this adaptation of *George Washington's Secret Six* with you. First and foremost, it's important to me that our latest generation of Americans understands how special our first generation was and how lucky we all are to be part of the American Miracle. I know I'm not alone in this hope. The most common refrain I get when I travel and speak about the original book is, "I wish my kids were old enough to read this story." Now there's an illustrated edition of it, just for you.

When you are born in the United States, you don't automatically know what makes America great. It's so difficult to be thankful and grateful for something you didn't do anything to earn. But understanding our past will help answer that question, and the story of the Culper Spy Ring is just the sort of history book I would have loved as a kid. It tells the fast-paced tale of true Patriots, showing a time of crisis when our sovereignty and security was threatened. And with so many seemingly impossible victories, you get the sense that perhaps divine intervention played a role in the founding of our nation.

Though George Washington lends his name to the title, the true message of this book is not to be more like him or to hold yourself to his standard. Our first president and first general is in a lofty category all his own. Rather, this is the story of so-called average, everyday Americans doing extraordinary things, putting their lives at risk for the hope of finding freedom, liberty, and a new country. The five men and one woman who formed the Culper Spy Ring—farmer Abraham Woodhull, longshoreman Caleb Brewster, tavern owner Austin Roe, grocer Robert Townsend, printer James Rivington, and female socialite Agent 355—accomplished feats that have even today's CIA in awe.

I believe we all can see ourselves in this story, and maybe we won't have to wait for another Marvel Comics movie to find our next superheroes. Real-life superheroes lived, and still live, right here in America. Maybe the next hero is your neighbor, your relative, your friend. Maybe it's you. All combined, we make the United States of America the finest country this world has produced, but unless you study our journey and relive our struggles, you will never truly appreciate it.

Enjoy!

Brian

Preface

Spring 1775

It could not have been a more exciting time for Patriots longing for liberty.

On April 19, on the town green in Lexington, Massachusetts, during a skirmish between colonial militiamen and British soldiers, a shot rang out. It was followed shortly after by another confrontation in nearby Concord. That one day would mark an indelible change in the course of history. It serves as the date on which to pin the beginning of the War of Independence. In 1837, it got its slogan, "the shot heard round the world," when Ralph Waldo Emerson published a poem called "Concord Hymn." Part of it reads:

> By the rude bridge that arched the flood,
> Their flag to April's breeze unfurled,
> Here once the embattled farmers stood
> And fired the shot heard round the world.

The colonists were soon to experience the true cost of war. On

Titled The Death of General Warren at the Battle of Bunker's Hill, June 17, 1775, *this painting was published in 1840 in a military magazine. It depicts famous soldiers on both sides of the conflict.*

June 17, 1775, on a hill outside of Boston, the ragtag colonial forces battered the British. But the Battle of Bunker Hill cost them heavy losses in life and limb for only a modest gain in land. The delegates from the colonies to the Second Continental Congress in Philadelphia knew that their forces could not withstand this kind of loss for long. Eventually, they would run out of people ready to fight.

The delegates urgently needed to prepare for a full-scale war. Among the representatives from Virginia was the tall, soft-spoken surveyor, farmer, and former spy widely regarded for his valor in battle and exemplary leadership in the militia during the previous war: George Washington.

That he was highly thought of is clear in this section of a letter John Adams wrote to his wife, Abigail:

> I can now inform you that the Congress have made Choice of the modest and virtuous, the amiable, generous and brave George Washington Esqr., to be the General of the American Army, and that he is to repair as soon as possible to the Camp before Boston.

It is also clear that Washington did not seek this task. The day after he was commissioned, he wrote to his wife, Martha, whom he called Patsy:

> It has been determined in Congress, that the whole army raised for the defense of the American Cause shall be put under my care, and that it is necessary for me to proceed immediately to Boston to take upon me the Command of it. You may believe me my dear Patsy, when I assure you in the most solemn manner, that, so far from seeking this appointment, I have used every endeavor in my power to avoid it.

Washington was a wise choice. What he lacked in soldiers and supplies, he made up for in intelligence. And his experience as a spy was to come in very handy in a short time.

General George Washington by Elkanah Tisdale, an American engraver and painter. The scene below the portrait imagines the moment on July 3, 1775, when Washington took command of the American army in Cambridge, Massachusetts. It was published in a military magazine in 1796.

George Washington's Army

George Washington had nerves of steel. He had led thousands of troops into battle, riding tall and calmly through even the heaviest fighting. Myths had grown up around the general; a few people said he was favored by God—that no arrows or bullets could harm him. Of course he was not actually untouchable, but he was regarded by his peers as a sober-minded man of vision, wisdom, humility, and experience. For these reasons Washington was asked to serve as the commander in chief of the Continental Army, also known as the Patriots, in their struggle to win independence from English rule.

But Washington knew that even substantial numbers of troops meant little without proper training and equipment, and his men lacked both. Washington had the utmost confidence in his officers, but to say that the rest of the Continental Army was rough around the edges would be an understatement. City men who had never held a rifle stood with country folk who had never had a day of formal schooling. Hardy farmers struggled to cooperate with young men of landed wealth who had never known a moment of discomfort or hunger in their lives. Old men lined up with boys who had lied about their age to join up in pursuit of adventure. They came from all over the country, from as far north as the mountains of New England and as far south as the swamps of Georgia.

Many of Washington's men had never been more than fifty miles from the place of their birth, let alone met anyone with such a

British ships fire on Bunker Hill in Charlestown, Massachusetts, as cannons in Boston join the attack. Charlestown is in flames. The image was published in a British history book around 1783.

strange accent as could be found in the hills of Virginia or the English settlements of Massachusetts. They were all on the side of liberty, but there the unity ended.

Despite the makeup of the army, it had enjoyed an early moral victory at Bunker Hill. The end of the Siege of Boston in March 1776, after almost a year, was also a win for the Patriots, but their success was due more to the position and strength of the American fortifications than to any great offensive maneuvers to rout the enemy. The British gave up on the city, leaving voluntarily rather than fleeing in an all-out retreat. General William Howe, then commander in chief of the British army in North America, had his sights set on a much bigger and more agreeable prize than belligerent Boston: the great port city of New York.

Although Washington knew he had the hearts of his men, and that most were brave, loyal, and passionate about their liberty, he did not know whether that passion could hold New York against the thousands of well-trained British forces decked out in their red-coated uniforms.

The few American troops still holding New York's Manhattan Island in 1776 were hanging on by a thread, and Washington was desperate to strengthen their position. To do so, he formulated a plan: he needed to recruit a spy to collect information on British plans. Espionage was not a new activity to Washington. He had served as a spy during the French and Indian War and knew how important it was to have advance information. At this stage in the war, with the troops he had, it was his only hope.

Washington saw that the Patriots would need to outmaneuver

the British; they could not overpower them. The British army and navy boasted superior numbers, training, supplies, and equipment, and there was little hope of defeating their forces in head-to-head combat—unless their battle plans and their weaknesses were already known. By learning the enemy's secrets, spies would play a crucial role in undermining British attacks, allowing the Continental Army to anticipate the redcoats' next moves.

Part One

CHAPTER 1

Why New York?

Holding New York was the cornerstone in Washington's strategy to win the war. The vast area included two islands (Staten Island and Manhattan Island), the western end of Long Island, and the territory north of Manhattan along the Hudson River. As the second-most populous city in the colonies, after Philadelphia, New York was an

This ink-and-watercolor drawing depicts New York City as seen from Long Island with the East River in the foreground. Most of the buildings are along the waterfront, leaving the rest of the land for farming and grazing animals. It is thought that the drawing was made in 1778 by John Montresor, a British military engineer.

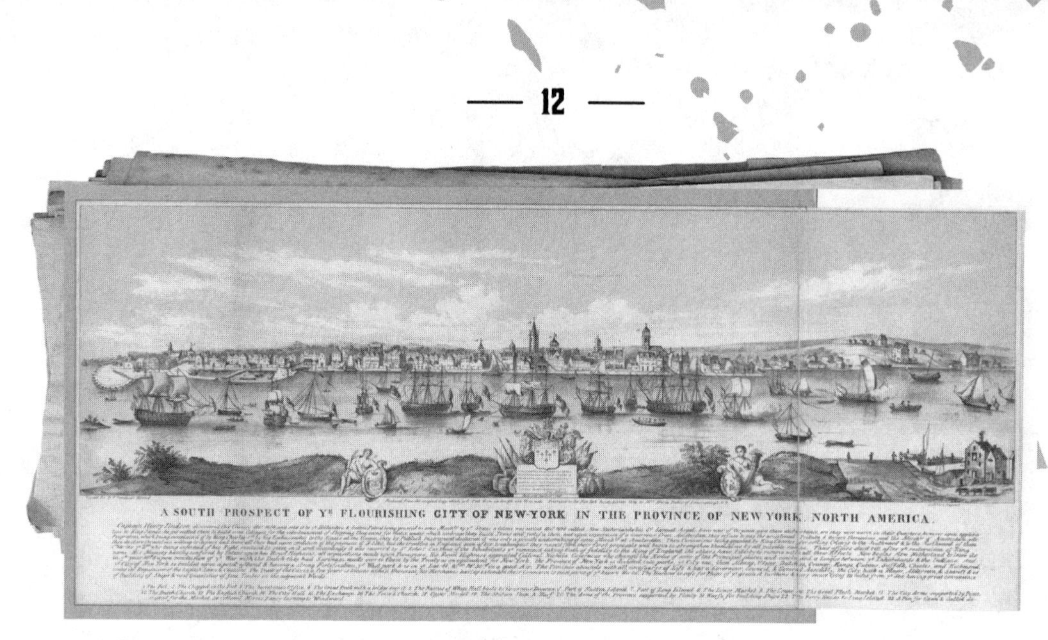

A lithograph from a pictorial history of the Revolution.

economic hub in the North. But even more significant were New York's location and situation—right in the center of Britain's North American settlements, with a large deepwater harbor and access to the Hudson River. The army that held New York City and its waterways had a strategic advantage not only in controlling the import and export of foodstuffs and dry goods but also in securing a key foothold for transporting troops up and down the coast.

Maintaining control of New York City and New York Harbor would give the American soldiers and the Patriot populace a tremendous boost in confidence, and it would certainly be an embarrassment to the British army and navy and to the many Loyalist citizens of New York. However, the British could survive such a blow. For the Americans, losing the region would be a tragedy, destroying morale, cutting off trade, and drastically lowering the odds that the Patriots could win the war.

CHAPTER 2

On the March

On April 4, 1776, Washington set out from his headquarters in Cambridge, Massachusetts. As he marched south, he must have nursed the hope that the Continental Army's muscle and moxie would be enough to outfight the British and hold Manhattan. Being a seasoned fighter and a brilliant strategist, he understood, perhaps better than anyone else in North America, that control of New York City was essential for the cause of liberty—and that keeping the city would be a daunting task.

Ten days later, Washington and his men arrived in Manhattan. Washington established his headquarters in a mansion. His men, ten thousand strong, slept where they could. That summer, news arrived that both cheered and sobered them all. Fifty-six delegates from the colonies had convened in the midst of stifling July heat in Philadelphia to form the Second Continental Congress, and had written and signed the Declaration of Independence, which stated

An illustration by Martha Lamb from a history of New York published in 1877. The text beneath it reads: "Viewing the half-ruined city of New York in the distance, Washington decided as well and wisely the course which would best contribute to her future greatness, as he could have done had he fully foreseen the glories of the coming century."

that the thirteen colonies sought to separate from England and become self-governing. If ever there was a point of no return, this was it.

The British, meanwhile, were amassing troops that would be twenty thousand strong on undefended Staten Island, with thirty thousand more on ships looming in New York Harbor.

As August dragged on, tensions mounted. A copy of the Declaration of Independence had been put before the Crown, which meant that King George III finally understood the seriousness of the colonists' determination to fight. No longer would King George order his generals to show restraint in their efforts to squelch the rebels or maintain that a mere show of force would be enough to subdue the Revolution. He would not show mercy. Of this Washington felt sure.

CHAPTER 3

Betrayal at Jamaica Pass

The first battle in the New York area was swift and devastating. Tipped off—perhaps by a spy within Washington's own ranks or by a Loyalist—that Jamaica Pass in Long Island was guarded by only five men, the British set out in that direction. The pass was part of a hilly, heavily wooded area that protected Brooklyn from attacks from the south.

General Sir William Howe. Howe was a viscount, the fourth level of the five levels of British noble peerage, which are, for men: duke, marquess, earl, viscount, and baron. For women, they are: duchess, marchioness, countess, viscountess, and baroness.

William Howard Jr., a young Patriot who ran a tavern with his father near Jamaica Pass, woke about two hours after midnight on the morning of August 27 to a British soldier standing beside his

This lithograph, called Howard's Inn, 1776, *depicts the building from which the guides were taken. A caption was later added to the original image that read, "Howard Halfway House, Atlantic & Alabama Avenue, East Brooklyn, destroyed 1902. Proprietor, coerced by Gen. Howe's forces, guided them to hill overlooking unguarded Jamaica Pass, making possible flanking maneuver that decided the Battle of Long Island in favor of the British, 1776." The image was created in 1866.*

bed. The soldier ordered him to get up, dress, and go downstairs. He quickly obeyed and found his father cornered by three redcoats pointing their muskets with fixed bayonets at him. A glance out the window revealed that a whole fighting unit stood at the ready.

General Howe himself waited for the two men in the barroom. "I must have some one of you to show me over the Rockaway Path around the pass," he remarked, setting down his empty glass.

"We belong to the other side, General," the father replied, "and can't serve you against our duty."

Howe's reply was kind but curt. "That is all very well; stick to your country or stick to your principles when you are free to do so. But tonight, Howard, you are my prisoner, and must guide my men over the hill."

The senior Howard began to protest, but Howe cut him off. "You have no alternative. If you refuse you will be shot."

The Howards directed General Howe up the winding footpath. Behind them marched ten thousand men, arriving at the other side in time to attack the Patriot General Nathan Woodhull and his men. As the battle continued throughout the day, Washington recognized his miscalculation: the full contingent of British troops would not storm Manhattan; the redcoats were bringing heavy force to bear on Brooklyn, too. Washington shifted more men and supplies to Brooklyn, but it was too late for the Americans to recover and hold their ground. By day's end, Brooklyn and the surrounding area were largely in British hands, with the retreating Patriots trapped in Brooklyn Heights. Manhattan was still held by the Continental Army, but Washington was sure it was only a matter of time until the British overtook it, too.

Washington's troops suffered a major blow. The Americans had lost more than 300 men that day, in addition to nearly 700 wounded and 1,000 captured. The British (and their hired German mercenaries, called Hessians) had lost a mere 64 men, with 31 reported as missing and 293 wounded.

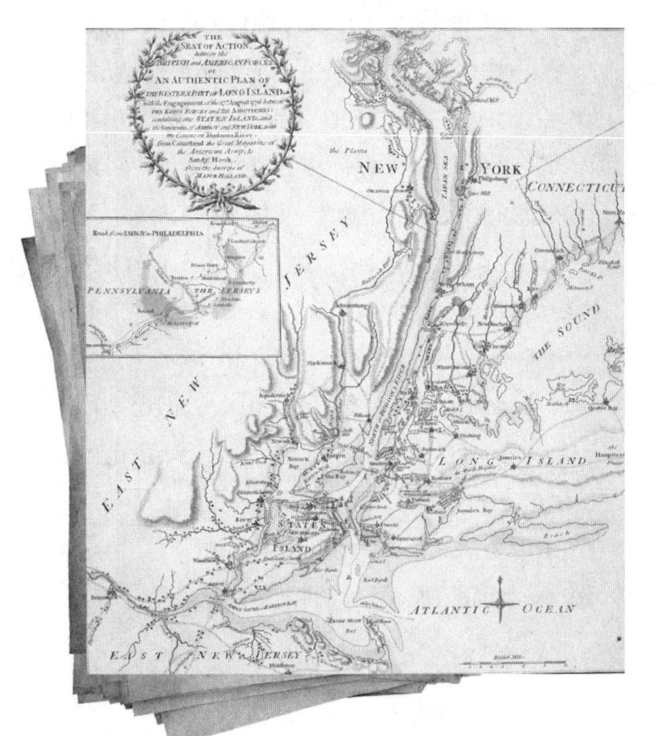

This map, drawn by Samuel Holland, the first surveyor general of British North America, is dated August 27, 1776. The small dots show locations of Patriot troops that Washington planted strategically along escape routes from New York City in anticipation of the British arrival. Unfortunately, he left Jamaica Pass unguarded.

CHAPTER 4

A Miracle in the Mist

Things could not have gone worse for the Continental Army. And it wasn't over, though the cannons had ceased firing for now. The fighting had taken Washington across the East River, and now he was essentially trapped in Brooklyn Heights, surrounded by the British and with no way to escape. If his troops pursued a retreat by land, they would walk directly into the British camps and either be shot on sight or captured and hanged for treason. If they took to the water to escape to Patriot-held Manhattan, they would be sitting ducks as the British fired cannonballs into their rowboats.

Just like that, the Revolution was all but over. Washington must have reeled at the turn of events. Maybe it was inevitable; after all, who were the colonists to think they had a chance against the mighty king of England and an empire that encircled the globe?

The Americans needed to get out and get out fast. Unless Washington could somehow ferry nine thousand men undetected across New York Harbor, currently patrolled by the might of the Royal Navy, he would be forced to surrender or ask his men to die in a siege from which there was no foreseeable escape.

Two days before the retreat across New York harbor, the American soldiers had been forced to retreat over the Gowanus Creek during the Battle of Brooklyn.

As night fell on the evening of August 29, Washington peered over New York Harbor and knew he had no other hope. Escape by water was the only chance—and even that would take a miracle. Ordering a hasty retreat, Washington oversaw the efforts to ferry his army and their possessions—every man, beast, cannon, and rifle—safely across the water under the cover of darkness. To his relief, the British sentinels failed to spot the shadowy silhouettes of the escaping soldiers. But as the sky began to lighten, there were still many men to move. Miraculously, a thick fog began to roll in, providing cover until every last soldier, animal, and piece of equipment reached safety on the other side. Washington's boots were the last to leave the Brooklyn Heights side of the harbor, and the last to alight in Manhattan.

By the time the fog lifted and the British realized what had happened, the Americans were already out of the reach of British cannons. They were down but not out. Washington knew it would be only a matter of days before General Howe ordered an attack on the remaining American fortifications in Manhattan, and that Manhattan would surely fall.

Moving north to Connecticut, Washington and his men rejoiced at their escape, though the all-but-complete loss of New York was a serious blow. Gone was the optimism created by the Boston victory. Troop morale was low. Backed into a corner, Washington now realized what every small, wily boy comes to recognize when faced with the brute strength of a schoolyard bully: he could not defeat his foe with manpower, arms, or any other show of force. He would have to beat the British in a battle of wits.

THE RETREAT FROM LONG ISLAND.

Washington directing the passage of the American Army across the East River, at night. The location is near the Brooklyn pier of the great bridge.

The retreat from Long Island under cover of darkness, as imagined and painted by Henry Alexander Ogden.

Part Two

CHAPTER 5

A Change in Strategy

As if the loss of most of New York wasn't bad enough, Washington's autumn was about to get worse. While the defeat at the Battle of Brooklyn had been a blow, the retreat had gone better than planned. Washington's next endeavor would not be so fortunate, ending instead in disaster. As he watched the British secure New York and received reports about the state of his army, Washington knew that his best hope was to out-spy the enemy.

Unfortunately for the rough-hewn Patriot army, spying required far more accuracy and delicacy than simply aiming a cannon, and it also took more time. Unlike waging a traditional battle, wherein two armies took a field and fired at each other for several hours or days until one side declared victory, gathering useful intelligence might take weeks or months before combat even began. Developing the sophistication and buying the time necessary to grow an effective spy ring would be difficult—especially in the locations where it mattered most.

Recognizing the difficulty of setting up a good espionage network, Washington shifted his wartime strategy from relying on nonexistent combat strength to placing his trust in intelligence gathering, even before the catastrophic loss of New York was complete. To begin, he needed one good man.

CHAPTER 6

One Good Man

The general needed a man to venture behind enemy lines disguised as a Loyalist. This man would make casual inquiries about troop movements and supply stores and send reports back to Washington. His work would inform the general's plans to take back New York City, its harbor, and the neighboring areas.

As the need for information became clear, Washington had asked Lieutenant Colonel Thomas Knowlton, a veteran of many battles and infiltrations, to assemble a select group of officers. On August 12, 1776, Knowlton met with the candidates to inform them of the need. Each was brave, each was trustworthy, and each was silent as Knowlton asked for a volunteer. Finally, twenty-one-year-old Nathan Hale stepped forward.

Hale had recently been given a lieutenant's commission by the Connecticut General Assembly. He was an amateur soldier, having taken part only in minor skirmishes. He was a teacher, an actor, and a passionate Patriot. And he was available right away.

A statue depicting Nathan Hale.

On Assignment

Washington immediately approved Hale's assignment. On September 12, the young man was ferried across the water from Stamford, Connecticut, to largely Loyalist Long Island. He would pose as a schoolmaster looking for work, a cover that would give him an excuse to meet leading townsmen and ask questions about the area.

But the move was too late. As September advanced, so had the British troops, capturing the lower end of Manhattan on September 15, just three days after Hale landed on Long Island. The defeat had been inevitable and Washington was prepared for the blow, but the timing could not have been worse.

Hale had little chance to establish his identity, let alone transmit any helpful intelligence to Washington, before the attack came on Manhattan. Now, every observation of British troop and supply movements would help Washington determine how to take back all of Manhattan, not simply defend their last stronghold on it. Hale was behind enemy lines. Any number of innocent situations could blow his cover to a suspicious local: an ignorance of the proximity of one town to the next, the mispronunciation of a word peculiar to that region, a slip of the tongue that would betray him as a mainlander.

Washington felt keenly the responsibility for Hale's safety, having had the final say on whether the mission would go forward. There was no way of knowing how the young man was coping, and this concerned Washington even more. Where was he staying? With whom was he speaking? Had he stumbled into any situations that might put him in harm's way? Just as much as he craved the information Hale would be sending, Washington wanted assurance that the young lieutenant had maintained his cover and could quietly exit Long Island when the right moment came.

By the time Hale landed, the island was full of redcoats armed and itching for a fight with anyone who had even a whiff of Patriot sentiments about him. But just as potentially damning to Hale's mission was the civilian population. While there were a few Patriots, the sympathies of most Long Islanders lay with King George. Even if a farmer was a Patriot, but a British military officer was living in his house, he was very likely to shout "God save the king!" if it kept his children safe and his fields unscathed. For this reason alone, Washington worried that a seemingly trustworthy contact might be tempted to report a suspected spy.

Hale's flimsy cover story might easily be blown: after all, what school would be looking for a teacher this far into September? Or maybe Hale's own Patriotic zeal would do him in, were he unable to remain silent in the face of insults to his cause or to resist sharing his true feelings with someone pretending to be a sympathetic ear.

A week passed with no disaster, and Washington breathed a sigh of relief. While the danger was still intense, he hoped Hale had established a solid cover and was out of direct suspicion. Unfortunately, his relief was premature.

CHAPTER 8

Failure on Long Island

On September 21, 1776, Washington spent most of the day studying maps and potential battle plans and, in the evening, writing a few letters. He had no way of knowing that at the tip of Manhattan, Nathan Hale was at that very moment being arrested, charged with spying, and sentenced to "be hanged by the neck until dead" the following morning.

As if to highlight Hale's lonely experience on Long Island, no one can say with certainty exactly where he was detected and captured, or even what activities he was engaged in before that fateful event. Somehow he made his way westward to Brooklyn, then crossed over into lower Manhattan, though no records show when or how. Perhaps he only made that crossing later, as a prisoner. By some reports, he was recognized by Loyalist cousins and reported to the British; by others, he mistook a British boat for the ferry sent to return him to safety; by still others, he was lulled into a false sense of safety and

A wood engraving showing the execution of Nathan Hale on September 21, 1776. It was published in the magazine Harper's Weekly *in 1860.*

shared the details of his plans with some Loyalist locals at a tavern and they turned him in. Whatever the case, he was captured, tried, and hanged all in the span of roughly twelve hours.

Shortly after Hale's body ceased to swing, Captain John Montresor of His Majesty's army set out for the American camp under a flag of truce. He was granted an audience with a young Patriot captain and aide to General Washington named Alexander Hamilton. Montresor informed the Americans of the execution of Lieutenant Hale. The visit was not only a formal courtesy but also a thinly veiled warning that their sad little attempt at espionage had been an embarrassing failure.

The news cut Washington deeply. Hale's death was a tragedy for its own sake, and for the fact that Washington now had no agent to feed him the information he desperately needed from Long Island. But while Hale's attempt to gather and convey intelligence had been an utter failure, he had given his general something valuable: the recognition that Washington needed more than just one brave man on Long Island; he needed an entire network.

CHAPTER 9

The March to New Jersey

As the autumn of 1776 progressed to winter, General George Washington found himself marching from New York to New Jersey to Pennsylvania in a series of disheartening campaigns. His troops were demoralized and the civilian population even more so. Many who were formerly enthusiastic supporters of the Patriot cause swore allegiance to the king or else quietly withdrew their support for liberty. In October, Washington met up with reinforcements, but found their number a mere half of the five thousand troops he had anticipated. Supplies were low, and he could no longer count on the local populace to show their support by selling food and other necessary supplies to the Continental Army. The British troops, on the other hand, were well supplied, and their numbers were bolstered by the Hessians, German mercenaries with a reputation for being tough and unflappable in battle.

Just before the celebration of Christmas, Washington was eyeing

George Washington watches his soldiers cross the Delaware River before the attack on Trenton. Soldiers, cannon, horses, and wagons all traveled on barges across the river. This painting by Thomas Sully was created in 1842 and published in the weekly newspaper New-York Mirror.

a return to New Jersey. He had to regain control of the mid-Atlantic after the disappointing autumn or he would lose the war, so he began to formulate a plan to attack the Hessian encampment at Trenton—a daring raid requiring yet another treacherous ferrying of men and supplies across water. Braving large masses of ice and winter winds that could easily overturn the small boats, his men would cross the Delaware River and capture the city in an attempt to break a stronghold of British control in the region.

Washington was cautiously optimistic that another miracle like the fog over New York Harbor would come to his aid. Because Washington had a secret.

CHAPTER 10

"There Will Be No Attack"

One evening, John Honeyman, a Scots-Irish immigrant who worked in Trenton as a butcher and a weaver, supposedly wandered too close to the Continental Army encampment. He was captured and interviewed by George Washington himself.

Honeyman "escaped" and returned to Trenton, where he made it known to a Hessian colonel that he had inside information. When the colonel asked if Washington's army looked ready to attack that night, Honeyman said no. The Hessians, now free to celebrate Christmas Eve, began to relax and eat and drink liberally.

Meanwhile, Honeyman quickly and quietly gathered his family and retreated eastward to New Brunswick, New Jersey . . . and Washington prepared to strike.

It had all been a beautifully orchestrated setup, from Honeyman's position in Trenton to his capture, escape, and meeting with the Hessian colonel. Honeyman was Washington's man. Learning from

Washington accepts the surrender of the Hessian mercenary soldiers at Trenton. The painting, by John Trumbull, is at the Yale School of Fine Arts.

Hale's death, the general had reached out to Honeyman earlier that fall, counting on his outstanding credentials from the French and Indian War, unshakable bravery, and unsuspicious occupation to enable him to operate undetected. Sure enough, Honeyman casually questioned and carefully counted the men about the city and offered a full report back to Washington. Washington asked his agent to plant the false story in the colonel's ear before spiriting himself and his family out of harm's way. "There will be no attack," Honeyman told a Hessian colonel. "The American troops are so disheartened and so bedraggled, they have no plans of advancing any time soon."

It was a perfect plan that went off without a hitch. Honeyman played his part beautifully, and the Hessian troops, all fighting massive hangovers from their raucous Christmas revelries, were caught completely off guard when the Patriots launched their attack in the early hours of December 26. The victory was swift, decisive, and crucial for the American cause.

Washington's espionage success further buoyed him and the troops. But the loss of Long Island and Manhattan still weighed heavily on the general's mind. He didn't think the war could be won without recapturing them, and like Trenton, they could not be taken without good, reliable intelligence. Honeyman's efforts at Trenton had proved the value of a well-placed spy and taught Washington two good lessons: his spies would have to blend in as Honeyman had (and Hale had not), and they would have to be absolutely convincing in their roles.

Washington would need a collection of agents—a ring of men and women with unquestionable fidelity and ordinary identities. He didn't want anyone who stood out. Washington's immediate task would be to enlist two key individuals: first, an officer familiar with the territory and well acquainted with the local families and customs, who could orchestrate the whole enterprise but remain close to Washington's side, and second, an agent on the ground who could recruit the other members, preferably a person who was well connected but had largely kept his political opinions to himself throughout the conflict—a man who would not raise suspicions, but who would rather die than surrender his liberties.

Washington inspects colors, also known as flags or standards, captured from the British at the battle of Trenton. Painting by Percy Moran around 1914.

CHAPTER 11

A Waiting Game

In January 1778, David Bushnell, an American inventor, devised a floating weapon. Kegs charged with gunpowder, dropped into the Delaware River near Philadelphia where the British were stationed, would explode if they bumped into anything. British seamen were engaged in shooting any debris that came near the kegs.

As 1777 led to 1778, George Washington's focus was, by necessity, pulled away from New York. Despite a devastating winter at Valley Forge, the Americans were no longer fighting alone, scraping out victories from sheer luck and pluck. Benjamin Franklin's negotiations in France had finally culminated in King Louis XVI's commitment to support the American cause. The Patriots had a well-equipped ally, although it would be many months before ships and troops arrived.

By June 1778, orders were issued for the British army in Philadelphia to abandon the city and set their sights on strengthening their all-important hold on New York.

Washington and his men prepared to follow suit, packing up the ragtag army to leave Valley Forge. The logistics of moving an army were all-consuming, but Washington was preoccupied with an even more important task: the time had come to focus his full attention on forming his spy network, and nothing would distract him now.

This illustration imagines an evening at Valley Forge. Note the strip of fabric that soldiers used to keep their ears from frostbite.

CHAPTER 12

The Brilliant Young Major: Benjamin Tallmadge

Washington needed someone who knew not only the city of New York and the various routes into and out of it but also enough trusted locals to recruit as spies. The candidate would also need to be nearly inexhaustible if he were to devote the time, strategy, and energy necessary to make the ring successful.

Fortunately for Washington, one of the rising young stars of the Continental Army fit the bill exactly. Benjamin Tallmadge, a gallant young major from Setauket on Long Island, was still rather green, but his keenness of mind was apparent to everyone who met him, and he knew how to earn the respect and faith of his men despite the occasional misstep. Besides, his demonstrated courage, his imagination, and, most important, his background made him the perfect candidate.

Major Benjamin Tallmadge, of the Second Continental Light Dragoons, was once thought to be a rather unlikely military man.

The son and grandson of ministers, young Benjamin seemed destined for the pulpit rather than the trenches.

He knew Nathan Hale in college and, like him, took part in theatricals there. The position of superintendent of the high school in Wethersfield, Connecticut, was offered to him after college, and Tallmadge seized the opportunity to share his enthusiasm for study with a younger generation. There, he served faithfully for three years, though his ambitions drew him toward the legal profession and he began to seriously consider studying law.

Benjamin Tallmadge.

But in the spring of 1775, "the shot heard round the world" rang out at Lexington, Massachusetts, followed by a skirmish at Concord a few hours later. Benjamin Tallmadge, like many young men of his time, was swept up in Patriotic fervor as the War of Independence officially began. Benjamin talked to friends who had been involved in the combat, and their stories of heroism and zeal began to shift Tallmadge's goal from fighting injustice in the courtroom to fighting tyranny on the battlefield.

In 1776, when the Second Continental Congress gave approval

for the colonies to actively expand their fighting brigades, Tallmadge took his leave of the high school at the end of the term and officially became a member of the Connecticut Continental Line on June 20.

Now a commissioned officer, Lieutenant Tallmadge distinguished himself with his boundless energy and uncanny knack for winning people over, but the art of war didn't come easily to the new recruit. With August came the fateful Battle of Brooklyn and the betrayal at Jamaica Pass. The battle was Tallmadge's first taste of war, and it shook him.

"This was the first time in my life that I had witnessed the awful scene of a battle, when man was engaged to destroy his fellow-man," Tallmadge wrote more than fifty years later. "I well remember my sensations on the occasion, for they were solemn beyond description, and very hardly could I bring my mind to be willing to attempt the life of a fellow-creature."

In mid-December 1776, Benjamin Tallmadge was promoted to captain of the Second Continental Light Dragoons by General George Washington himself, who had admired the young man's abilities and conduct, not to mention his loyalty. The appointment was signed in the unmistakable hand of John Hancock, and Tallmadge accepted it willingly. He devoted the first third of 1777 to training men and horses for scouting missions and light raids ahead of the more heavily armed cavalry and artillery brigades.

During the brutal winter of 1777 and into January 1778, Tallmadge stayed close to George Washington at Valley Forge; in such cramped and miserable quarters, the young officer impressed his commander. He was still somewhat untested and not always as farsighted as more seasoned officers, but both his input and his unsinkable enthusiasm were valued by both subordinates and superiors.

When Washington tapped him to act as spymaster on Long Island, Tallmadge acted quickly. He knew right away whom he would approach to be his man on the ground.

CHAPTER 13

The Black Sheep: Abraham Woodhull

Growing up, Abraham Woodhull was a neighbor of Benjamin Tallmadge's, and he shared many of the young officer's ideals, but that's where their resemblance ended. Woodhull was not a bright-eyed, optimistic, jolly-young-man-turned-soldier like Tallmadge. He agreed with the desire for liberty, but he wanted so badly to be personally independent that he avoided official military service because he would have been subject to the orders of superiors.

Abraham was his parents' third son, raised in a prominent and celebrated family. While his older brothers, Richard V and Adam, were groomed to step into the role of American gentlemen and succeed their father, young Abraham was released to the freedom of the outdoors. He neither minded nor resented his lot in life, especially since he found schoolwork hard and boring. While his brothers were laboring over passages of classical literature, Abraham explored the landscape of Long Island.

British troops set off for Long Island. Created in 1870 by the engraver John Karst, this image gives a good impression of the British troop strength that was dedicated to defending their position in New York.

The Woodhull girls, Susannah and Mary, doted on their baby brother, and Abraham was equally fond of them. When Mary married Amos Underhill and moved with him to Manhattan, Abraham made a habit of visiting them. Sometimes he traveled by land across Long Island and then by boat across the East River to Manhattan. Other times he caught a ride with a longshoreman rowing across Long Island Sound to Connecticut and then traveled southward over land to the city. He enjoyed these trips, but he was not free for long. In 1768, at the age of twenty-one, Adam died; six years later, at the age of thirty, Richard V died. And so, in 1774, Abraham found himself suddenly and unexpectedly in position to inherit the Woodhull family's homestead.

It was a windfall he had neither hoped for when it was out of reach nor welcomed now that it was his. He had never considered himself cut from the same fabric as the rest of the prominent landowners in his father's circle, and had gone to some pains not to adopt their upright and uptight behavior. Abraham Woodhull was proud of being the black sheep of his straitlaced family, and so he assumed the burden of familial duty with reluctance.

CHAPTER 14

Setting Up Aliases

How Tallmadge and Woodhull reconnected and developed the first phase of their plan is not exactly clear. It is almost certain that Tallmadge arranged to meet his old neighbor and family friend in Connecticut, as the risk of setting foot in occupied New York City or Long Island would have been too great. Most of Connecticut was still solidly in American hands in August 1778, providing a good meeting place for the two men.

Woodhull was appealing as a recruit because Tallmadge knew that he could be trusted, that he was a skilled judge of character and would enlist the aid of good men, and that he was a Patriot.

Tallmadge informed Woodhull of his charge from Washington. He was to install a ring of spies to convey information from Manhattan, either directly by land over the border to Connecticut or, perhaps more safely, across the Sound from Long Island and from there to the more rural areas of Connecticut (much farther from British inspectors who might possibly intercept the intelligence). Tallmadge, who was based in Connecticut, would receive and analyze the sensitive information before spiriting it away to wherever Washington happened to be encamped at the time, which was almost always within just a few days' ride of New York City. Tallmadge wanted Woodhull to find the spies from among his community on Long Island because they were the people who knew the land, the water, and the local customs.

Woodhull agreed.

A few days later, Tallmadge met with Washington in White Plains, New York. Of utmost importance to both was the creation of pseudonyms. The stakes were far too high for Tallmadge and Woodhull to use their real names in any kind of correspondence. In Tallmadge's case, an intercepted letter would make him an even higher-value target should the British learn he was now a spy. In Woodhull's case, living in the midst of the enemy, identification meant immediate arrest, likely followed by a trip to the gallows.

The general and the major discussed the best approach to the assignment of names—at once specific enough to be clearly and instantly identifiable to the intended recipient, yet not so unusual as to be obviously fake, nor so common that an innocent individual who happened to bear the same name might be hunted down by the enemy. Thus, Tallmadge was dubbed "John Bolton," using one of the oldest surnames in the colonies. The origin of Woodhull's name was a little more creative. Tallmadge selected "Samuel" for a first name, probably in honor of his younger brother, Samuel Tallmadge, who had done some courier work for Patriot efforts on Long Island. The last name, it has been suggested, was an adaptation of "Culpeper," a county in Virginia near Washington's boyhood home. Thus, "Samuel Culper" was born.

The pseudonyms were in place. Courier routes were set. Specifics as to the type of information Washington sought were established. The groundwork was laid for the ring to begin its work. The first two cogs, Tallmadge and Woodhull, could now begin turning the wheel that would steadily roll out the defeat of the British in New York. They would not disappear into their new identities and leave their old lives behind. Instead, their spy names would serve as their passports into a double life—with Tallmadge as an intelligence officer with a closely guarded secret and a covert post in Connecticut where he would retrieve the latest news, and Woodhull as a man who must go unnoticed in the den while seeking ways to overthrow the lions.

CHAPTER 15

A Bull of a Man: Caleb Brewster

Woodhull had his sights set on Caleb Brewster as a fellow spy from the beginning. Brewster was also from Long Island and had signed a statement saying he would support the Patriots. As a longshoreman, he was a bull of a man—physically huge and imposing from his work of loading and unloading cargo from ships. Recently he had taken to using his intimidating size and tremendous athletic skill to make himself a regular nuisance to the British. Ever the daredevil, he taunted them from his boat laden with smuggled goods and then amazingly evaded capture. Just as Woodhull knew the landscape, Brewster knew the coves and the waterways of Long Island Sound, slipping out of reach of the British by ducking into one or another until the patrol gave up trying to catch him.

What Woodhull did not know was that Brewster had already embraced the thrill of espionage. The young man had been in correspondence with General Washington since July 1778—several

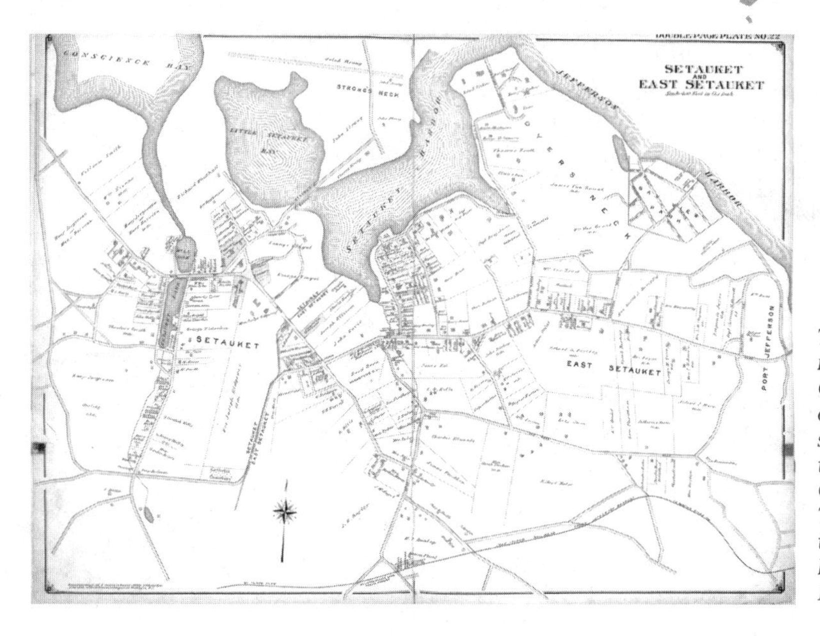

The bays and inlets near Setauket gave Caleb Brewster ample opportunity both to spy on the British and to stealthily set off for Connecticut and return. The area just north of the map border is the huge expanse of Long Island Sound.

weeks before Tallmadge had recruited Woodhull to manage the ring—reporting on the state of the British warships in New York Harbor, as well as on troop movements and naval preparations around Long Island. His reports revealed little new information and were somewhat out-of-date by the time they reached Washington, but the gesture proved to the commander in chief that there were Patriots ready and willing to spy and that a well-organized ring of secret agents could yield real intelligence.

While taking care not to be overheard, Woodhull was probably rather direct in his proposal to Brewster. The youth's vigor and fearlessness in openly defying the British navy on the Sound left little doubt where his sentiments lay. Already hooked on the adrenaline rush of espionage, Brewster was an easy sell. He enthusiastically agreed to ferry messages to Connecticut and even offered to add his own observations to the reports headed to Tallmadge.

CHAPTER 16

The Tavern Keeper: Austin Roe

Woodhull supposed that his old friend Austin Roe might prove more difficult to recruit. But Roe could provide one essential element to the group: he owned a tavern in East Setauket on Long Island that was patronized by British soldiers and other people loyal to the king. Roe was friends with Brewster, both jovial and spirited. In addition, Roe was comfortably situated, married, and firmly established in his business—and he didn't seem to have the daredevil streak that Brewster had. He couldn't afford it. His livelihood was entirely dependent upon the loyal patronage of local folks, many of them Loyalists, and the occasional traveler who passed his way and needed a room for the night.

His work made overhearing enemy conversations an easy task. However, because he was in the public eye, he had to be especially careful. Suspicions have a way of becoming whispers in small towns, and rumors about Roe's activities could hurt his business even after the war. Of course, should the spies' work be discovered, they could all expect something far worse than a loss of employment.

Despite initial concerns, Roe was pleased by the mission and eager to offer his service in any way he could.

Austin Roe's tavern as it looks today. It was a large building for the time, meant to have rooms and dining areas for travelers, as well as private areas for the family.

CHAPTER 17

Breaking from Tradition: A New Way to Work a Spy Ring

Now a team of three, Woodhull, Brewster, and Roe devised a plan by which their intelligence would crisscross its way over land and water to reach General Washington. Woodhull would operate from his brother-in-law Amos Underhill's boardinghouse in Manhattan, a location unlikely to arouse suspicion because he already made fairly regular visits. The information he gathered would leave the city in one of two ways. Either Roe would make the trip into the city on the pretense of purchasing supplies for his tavern, or Woodhull himself would travel back to Setauket, where he would leave the papers at Roe's tavern or a predetermined location in a field near Roe's house. This "dead-drop" method was less likely to raise suspicions but presented a much higher risk of a stranger's stumbling upon the papers before they had been picked up, so the men rarely employed it.

The Woodhull and Roe families were known to be old friends—

Roe's father had purchased the building he used for his home and business from the Woodhulls back in 1759—so nothing would seem out of place even if the two men were seen together carrying letters for the folks at home or visiting in the city. But Roe and Woodhull took care to ensure that the patterns of their meetings would not become too predictable and therefore seem shady to nosy locals or eagle-eyed British soldiers.

Caleb Brewster, whose family lived just yards away from Roe, would wait for an opportunity to retrieve the papers from Roe. He would then row across Long Island Sound when the British navy had their backs turned. On the Connecticut side of the Sound, Tallmadge would be waiting for Brewster to dock and pass off the letters, which Tallmadge would then hand-deliver to the general.

The whole process usually took approximately two weeks from beginning to end. The plan offered important advantages over the more traditional method of a single spy slipping in to gather intelligence and then slipping back out again. Local people were less likely to raise suspicions than an outsider who suddenly appeared in the town, skulked about for a few days, and then disappeared again. The intermediate step of entrusting the papers to Roe was a brilliant one. It minimized the connection between Woodhull's frequent trips to the city—as well as his extended stays there—and Brewster's regular dashes across the water, and it allowed the men to avoid apparent contact. The proximity of Brewster's home to Roe's made their familiarity far more natural.

CHAPTER 18

The Reports Begin

Almost immediately, Woodhull revealed himself to be a remarkably careful observer, detailing where British troops were situated and how strong their positions were, but he was also an extremely nervous operative. On November 23, 1778, Woodhull as Culper wrote to General Washington with a precise count of troops at various towns on Long Island, as well as a request for reimbursement for his expenses.

Washington was impressed with the detailed information he received and spoke with Tallmadge about arranging a face-to-face meeting with his brave new ringleader—a suggestion that rattled Woodhull no small amount. He thought he had made it abundantly clear to Tallmadge that he did not want his association with spying activities to be openly acknowledged in any public way. Of course, the general knew about the ring, but Woodhull felt that his personal appearance before Washington was unnecessary and would raise questions.

The proposed meeting was abandoned, but Woodhull remained nervous. His agitation was not improved by a slight adjustment made to the delivery route just five weeks later, in January 1779. Instead of Tallmadge personally delivering the letters to General Washington's hand, he was now going to pass them off to General Israel Putnam, who would then carry them and other dispatches from Danbury, Connecticut, to wherever the commander in chief was encamped at the time. Even though Putnam, a hero of Bunker Hill, knew nothing of the true identity of Culper, it was nerve-racking for Woodhull, who feared any involvement of strangers.

Austin Roe also made a move that rankled Woodhull even further: he hired a young man named Jonas Hawkins as an occasional courier, both to dilute suspicion and to get information into Tallmadge's hands more quickly, because Hawkins could carry information at times when Roe's business prevented him from traveling. Even if Hawkins was not privy to the full extent of the operation, another person now knew at least part of the secret, and this worried Woodhull. But the changes halved the amount of time it took for Woodhull's intelligence to reach Washington, from two weeks to only one. Woodhull couldn't argue against the improvement.

Despite his fraying nerves, Woodhull persisted with his meticulous scouting reports. Caleb Brewster supplemented the reports with his own reporting on shipbuilding activities and the particular ships in each Long Island inlet and harbor.

Together, these reports began to create a rich and detailed picture of New York's defenses, as well as providing important clues about the enemy's future strategy.

CHAPTER 19

The Unbreakable Code

As the spring of 1779 crept into New York, Woodhull was near panic, obsessed with the fear that he was on the verge of being found out and arrested. There was one promising development, however, which gave Woodhull a sense of relief: the long-awaited arrival of a particular concoction that promised to give him an added layer of security. Washington had obtained a supply of invisible ink and issued Woodhull a vial of the precious substance for the writing of the Culper reports.

The practice of writing with disappearing inks was nothing new. For centuries people had been communicating surreptitiously through natural and chemically manipulated inks that became visible when exposed to heat, light, or acid. By the eighteenth century it was common practice to expose—via these methods—letters suspected to contain secret information, in an effort to reveal any hidden content written in "white ink." Secret correspondence in the British military often had a subtle *F* or *A* in the corner, indicating to the recipient whether the paper should be exposed to fire or acid.

But the usefulness of these devices was limited because they were all so well known. Washington wanted something innovative and unknown to the British, and he received such a solution from a statesman and spymaster of the Hudson Valley named John Jay. Jay's older brother had developed an ink that only became visible through the application of a specific "sympathetic stain." Both the ink and the stain required a complicated recipe and special workshop, and they were extremely difficult to manufacture in any great quantity, so they were valuable commodities.

When Washington received his first batch of the ink, he was delighted with the effect. It was, in a way, an unbreakable code, impervious to any of the usual means of discovery. Even if the British suspected a white-ink message in any particular letter, they had no way of revealing it unless they, too, possessed the stain necessary to see the writing.

That small vial of ink must have been a huge relief to Woodhull. He had been waiting for its arrival for months, ever since the ink's existence was first mentioned to him, aware of how sparing he must be with its use and yet eager to entrust all of his gathered reports to its protection. He could hardly wait to begin writing back to Washington all that he was witnessing as New York began to thaw from another long winter.

CHAPTER 20

Panic and a Traitor

Woodhull's enthusiasm was short-lived. While he was away in New York City collecting information, British soldiers surrounded his home, questioned his family, and beat his father when they couldn't find Abraham. A prisoner of the British had named Abraham Woodhull as a spy. Washington took pity on Woodhull and asked him to recruit a substitute.

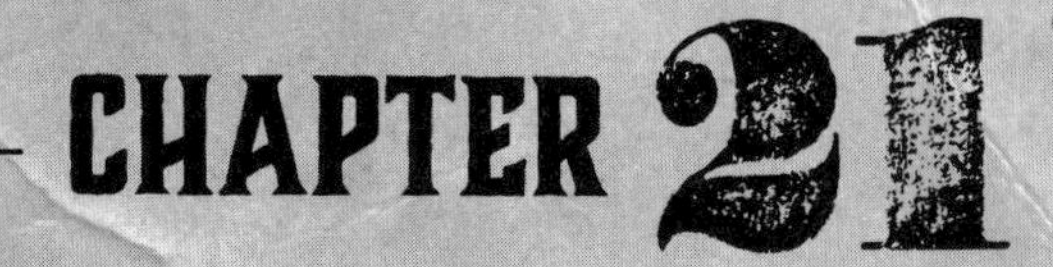

CHAPTER 21

The Peaceable Man: Robert Townsend

Robert Townsend was a quiet boy from a prominent Oyster Bay, Long Island, family with a history of independent thinking, which he had inherited. A peaceable man, he did his best to stay out of the war—until one event forced him to take a stand.

Townsend ran a modest dry goods shop in lower Manhattan, now solidly in British hands. He prospered in the midst of the enemy by being unobtrusive and trying to stay out of political discussions. But all people have breaking points, moments when they have seen one atrocity too many, weathered one insult too many, stayed still for one day too long—and they know they

This sketch is the only likeness of Robert Townsend. The artist and occasion are unknown.

British governor George Clinton's house on Pearl Street in Manhattan in 1775. The arcade covering the first floor offered shade and relief from dust to the rooms behind it. Although created in 1903, this image most likely reflects what the area looked like.

must act or hate themselves for keeping silent.

For Robert Townsend, that moment arrived in the fall of 1778. As Abraham Woodhull and his initial ring were beginning their intelligence war against the British in Manhattan and Long Island, the occupying armies were settling comfortably in various private residences, including the Homestead, Robert Townsend's beloved home in Oyster Bay.

Lieutenant Colonel John Simcoe, the man who had ordered the beating of Woodhull's father, decided that the Townsend family's house, one of the more comfortably situated and furnished dwellings in the town, fit his purposes quite nicely. He proceeded to set up his headquarters in the main part of the home, letting the family use just a few back rooms. At Simcoe's orders, British troops destroyed the orchard, of which Robert's father had been so proud, to feed British fires and help build a fort. The town operated as if under martial law, with roughly 470 enemy soldiers quartering there, including Hessian mercenary squads that roamed the streets to make sure residents stayed indoors at night. There were public lashings for those who displeased the soldiers, and little recourse for those who brought complaints. The town was quickly descending into a simmering chaos, and any lingering Loyalist feelings among the good people of Oyster Bay were rapidly evaporating.

British Lieutenant Colonel John Simcoe.

When Robert returned home in November 1778 to visit his family, he was no doubt shocked by his father's defeated appearance and posture. There were too many soldiers around to dare publicly voice any dissatisfaction with the current state of things, but tales of hardship and abuse were recounted in hushed tones and with sideways glances to check for British ears. Robert burned with anger as he learned of the liberties taken with neighbors' properties and lives. He could only stare in mute fury as he observed how the soldiers, including Colonel Simcoe himself, flirted openly with his sisters under their father's roof.

The Townsend family stood as much chance of evicting Simcoe from their property as they did of expelling the whole enemy encampment from Long Island. They were in British-held territory, so British laws stood and protesters fell—or were hanged.

When Robert returned to his shop in Manhattan, he was haunted by what he had seen. It is possible that the notion of spying had already crossed Robert Townsend's mind before Abraham Woodhull entered his shop in the late spring of 1779. It may have already been clear to Townsend that his position in the city gave him access to potentially valuable information. After all, he was privy to scraps of conversation between soldiers in his own shop, could note the flow of supplies and men into and out of the harbor as he inspected his own shipments on the docks, and could observe the habits and patterns of the higher-ranking officers who graced James Rivington's posh new coffeehouse just down the street. But even if such an idea had introduced itself to his mind, it may not have been a welcome thought or one that he relished. And even if he had been eager to undertake such an effort, he would have had no channel for it, no clearly defined plan for how to get such information into the hands of those to whom it meant something—until he found himself across the table from the old acquaintance who now offered him a new mission and a new name: Samuel Culper, Jr.

The two men talked long into the night, discussing every eventuality, every risk, and every pressing reason why these risks didn't ultimately matter. Woodhull would add "Senior" to his code name, and Townsend would become "Culper Junior." No one need ever know—nor even have the means to discover—the real man behind the intelligence reports.

Woodhull's earlier desire for anonymity now paled in comparison to that of Townsend, who insisted that no one other than Woodhull and the courier—not even General Washington—should be aware of his involvement. Townsend was leery even of the courier knowing his face, but relented out of necessity.

Woodhull wrote to Washington on June 20:

> My success hath exceeded my most sanguine expectations. I have communicated my business to an intimate friend. . . . It was with great difficulty I gained his complyance, checked by fear. He is a person that hath the interest of our Country

at heart and of good reputation, character and family as any of my acquaintance. I am under the most solomn obligations never to disclose his name to any but the Post, who unavoidably must know it. I have reason to think his advantages for serving you and abilities are far superior to mine.

Business and residential buildings in Manhattan edged the river on each side. This area is very near the offices of the newspaper Rivington owned.

CHAPTER 22

Washington's Orders

General Washington was delighted with the proposal and, together with Tallmadge, drafted a detailed list of guidelines and directives for his new agent in New York. The full document, below, offers an intimate perspective on Washington's philosophies regarding spying, and the specific mission of Culper Junior:

> **INSTRUCTIONS.**
> C—— Junr, to remain in the City, to collect all the useful information he can—to do this he should mix as much as possible among the officers and Refugees, visit the Coffee Houses, and all public places. He is to pay particular attention to the movements by land and water in and about the city especially. How their transports are secured against attempt to destroy them—whether by armed vessels upon the flanks, or by chains, Booms, or any contrivances to keep off fire Rafts.

The number of men destined for the defence of the City and Environs, endeavoring to designate the particular corps, and where each is posted.

To be particular in describing the place where the works cross the Island in the Rear of the City—how many Redoubts are upon the line from River to River, how many Cannon in each, and of what weight and whether the Redoubts are closed or open next the city.

Whether there are any Works upon the Island of New York between those near the City and the works at Fort Knyphausen or Washington, and if any, whereabouts and of what kind.

To be very particular to find out whether any works are thrown up on Harlem River, near Harlem Town, and whether Horn's Hook is fortifyed. If so, how many men are kept at each place, and what number and what sized Cannon are in those works.

To enquire whether they have dug Pits within and in front of the lines and Works in general, three or four feet deep, in which sharp pointed stakes are fixed. These are intended to receive and wound men who attempt a surprise at night.

The state of the provisions, Forage and Fuel to be attended to, as also the Health and Spirits of the Army, Navy and City.

These are the principal matters to be observed within the Island and about the City of New York. Many more may occur to a person of C—— Junr's penetration which he will note and communicate.

C—— Senior's station to be upon Long Island to receive and transmit the intelligence of C—— Junior.

As it is imagined that the only post of consequence which the enemy will attempt to hold upon Long Island in case of attack will be at Brooklyn, I would recommend that some inhabitant in the neighborhood of that place, and seemingly in the interest of the enemy, should be procured, who might probably gain daily admission into the Garrison by carrying on marketing, and from him intelligence might be gained every day or two of what was passing within, as the strength of the Garrison, the number and size of the Cannon, &c.

Proper persons to be procured at convenient distances along the Sound from Brooklyn to Newtown whose business it shall be to observe and report what is passing upon the water, as whether any Vessels or Boats with troops are moving, their number and which way they seem bound.

There can be scarcely any need of recommending the greatest Caution and secrecy in a Business so critical and dangerous. The following seem to be the best general rules:

To intrust none but the persons fixed upon to transact the Business.

To deliver the dispatches to none upon our side but those who shall be pitched upon for the purpose of receiving them and to transmit them and any intelligence that may be obtained to no one but the Commander-in-Chief.

Washington thought Brooklyn was the one place on Long Island that the British would regard as indispensable. Because the Culper Ring's route of conveying messages passed directly from Manhattan to Brooklyn, before continuing on to Setauket and across the Sound to Connecticut, the courier would have an excellent opportunity to observe military activity in Brooklyn and could add any relevant information to the letter he was carrying from Townsend. In short, the route seemed as close to an ideal arrangement as Washington could hope for at the time.

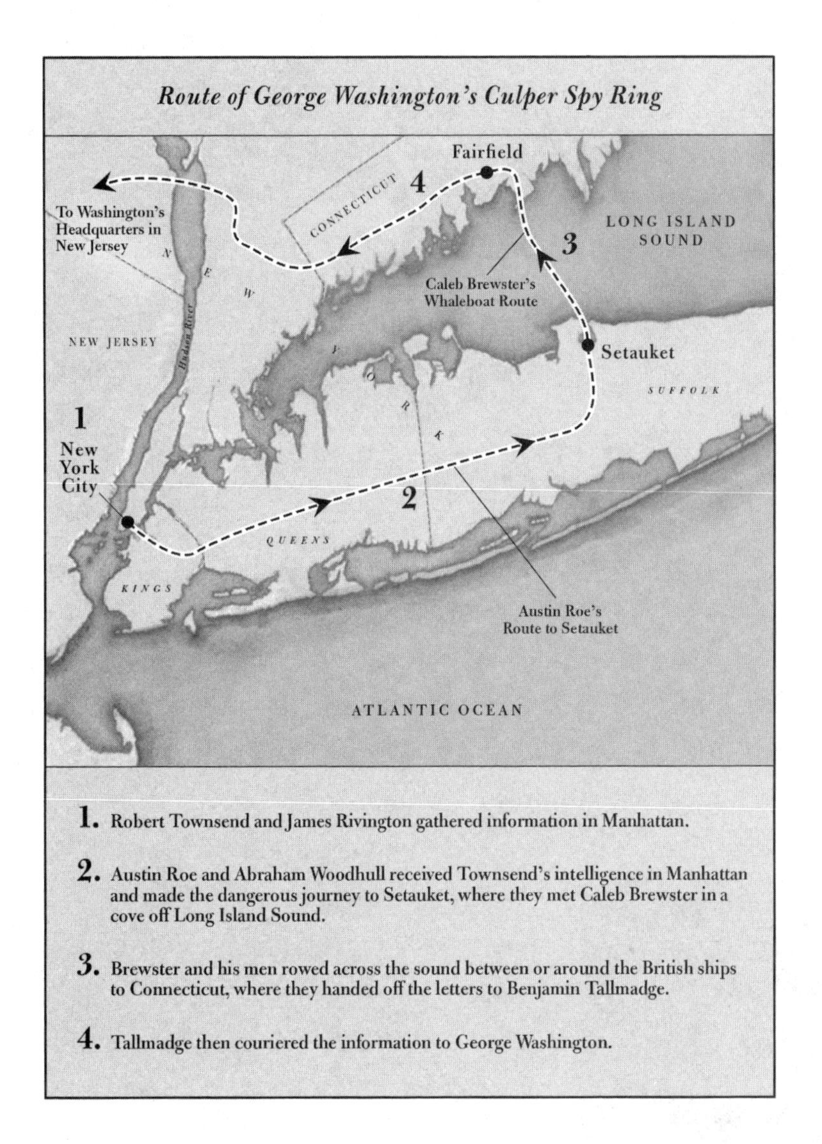
Route of George Washington's Culper Spy Ring
Fairfield
4
CONNECTICUT
To Washington's Headquarters in New Jersey
LONG ISLAND SOUND
3
Caleb Brewster's Whaleboat Route
NEW JERSEY
Hudson River
Setauket
SUFFOLK
1
New York City
2
QUEENS
KINGS
Austin Roe's Route to Setauket
ATLANTIC OCEAN
1. Robert Townsend and James Rivington gathered information in Manhattan.
2. Austin Roe and Abraham Woodhull received Townsend's intelligence in Manhattan and made the dangerous journey to Setauket, where they met Caleb Brewster in a cove off Long Island Sound.
3. Brewster and his men rowed across the sound between or around the British ships to Connecticut, where they handed off the letters to Benjamin Tallmadge.
4. Tallmadge then couriered the information to George Washington.

This map shows the general route the spies took to get messages from Manhattan to General Washington's headquarters in the field.

CHAPTER 23

The Cover Story: James Rivington

Robert Townsend's career as a spy began in that summer of 1779. His fears of the courier knowing his identity proved largely needless: Woodhull himself (at least at first) seems to have been the primary person who retrieved Townsend's reports to begin their circuitous route to General Washington.

Townsend soon felt he needed a way to move more freely about the city, making inquiries and giving people a reason to trust him. In other words, he needed a cover story, and he found one just down the street, in the coffeehouse and print shop of an English expatriate named James Rivington. In 1773, Rivington had started publishing his own newspaper as a neutral press with the tagline "Open and Uninfluenced," but eventually the

James Rivington.

paper began to promote (as did so many newspapers of the era) a very specific and forceful worldview. In Rivington's case, it was loyalty to King George. Recognizing the possibility for a perfect cover story, Townsend applied for a job at Rivington's paper to write the occasional column of local interest. Rivington recognized the quiet shopkeeper from down the street and was happy to take him up on his offer to contribute to the *Royal Gazette*.

A coffeehouse much like the one James Rivington owned.

It was a stroke of brilliance on Townsend's part. He now had the perfect excuse for asking questions, jotting down details, and questioning movements of troops and supplies into, out of, and around the city. What was more, Rivington's Loyalist politics would help deflect any suspicion that Townsend might be harboring Patriotic sentiments.

Another, more sinister figure was establishing himself at Rivington's coffeehouse at the same time, however. The British had wasted no time in developing their own spy network. In the spring of 1779, General Henry Clinton, the new commander in chief of the British army in America, had appointed the dashing young major John André as his chief intelligence officer. The major had impressed the general with his wit and savvy when the general arrived in Philadelphia in the

John André.

early months of 1778. Now, a little over a year after they first became acquainted, Clinton entrusted André with the task of managing British espionage efforts in the colonies, with a specific eye on New York. André and Clinton were well aware that Washington was desperate to retake New York and had to be sending spies there. Eager to intercept Patriot agents, the new intelligence officer set up his headquarters in Manhattan.

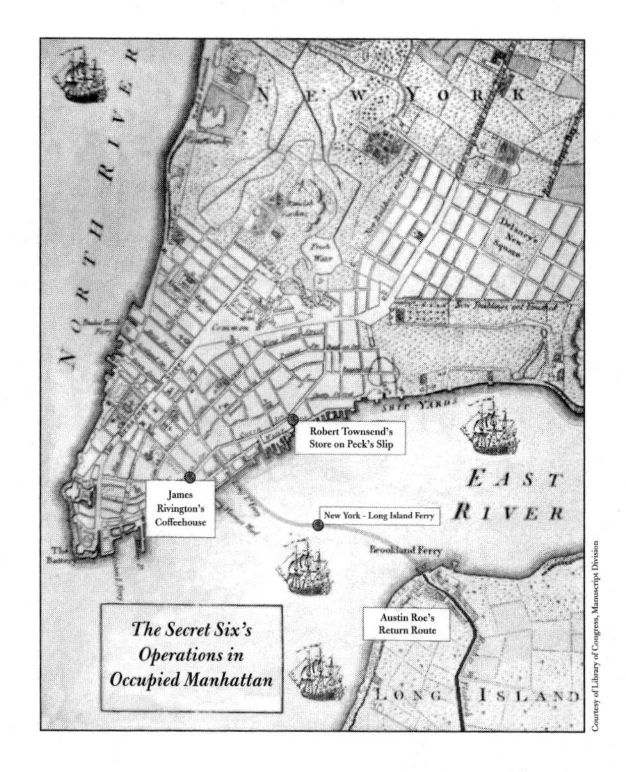

Robert Townsend's business was just a few blocks from James Rivington's office. The Long Island ferry dock is conveniently between the two.

CHAPTER 24

The Mysterious Lady

In his letter to Tallmadge dated August 15, 1779, Woodhull recorded that there was a specific "[lady] of my acquaintance" so situated as to "out wit them all." Her sudden appearance in his letters following the recruitment of Townsend, as well as the fact that Townsend's shop ledger shows he and Woodhull met that same day, hints that she may have been introduced to the ring by Townsend himself. That she was already of Woodhull's acquaintance indicates that her name, at least, was already known to him prior to that day, perhaps indicating that she or her family were originally from Long Island. But her apparent presence in Manhattan of late meant that she was somehow uniquely positioned to collect important secrets in a cunning and charming manner that would leave her marks completely unaware that they had just been outwitted by a secret agent.

But who was this mysterious woman so perfectly poised

to steal such vital secrets? Woodhull was careful not to record her name, offering only a number—355—in the code that was to define the Culper Ring. The identity of Agent 355 remains a mystery to this day.

In two languages, French and German, this image celebrates the entrance of the British troops into New York. Created by Franz Xaver Habermann, it is thought to have been published in 1778 in Germany.

CHAPTER 25

Hiding in Plain Sight

Several close calls involving captured letters had made the creation of a code essential for the Culper Ring. The spy ring had already begun to use a few numerical substitutions in their letters: for example, 10 stood for New York and 20 for Setauket, so that the recipient would know the source of the information contained in the reports. Two additional numbers, 30 and 40, were used to designate Jonas Hawkins and Austin Roe as post riders delivering the messages to their next destination. Tallmadge now realized how essential it was to develop a more complete code dictionary and to assign every member or associate of the ring a number rather than just a code name. In a style of cryptography developed originally by the French, Tallmadge selected a book and got to work. He chose Entick's New Spelling Dictionary, the 1777 London edition. First, using the dictionary, he made a list of all the words he thought the ring would need to use to communicate. Then he added people's names, local places, and other words. Finally, his list was 763 words long. He assigned each word, location, or name a number from 1 to 763. He became 721, Woodhull as Culper Senior 722, Townsend as Culper Junior 723, Roe 724, and Brewster 725. General Washington was 711, and his British counterpart, General Clinton, was 712. Numbers were represented by letters, so that the year 1779, for example, would read as "ennq." If a word needed to be made plural, or put in the past or future tense, a "flourish" would be written on top of it to designate the change.

The new system was not foolproof and required some adjustments on the part of the users, but Woodhull and Tallmadge were able to use it to correspond comfortably within a few weeks.

The Patriot spies and their superiors investigated many ways of sending messages. Washington advocated hiding messages in plain view. If a letter was treated with the utmost caution and concern, it was more likely to appear suspicious and tip off British inspectors. If instead the spies passed along highly sensitive information hidden in a book or disguised as dull letters on day-to-day family news, the vehicle by which the message was being sent would probably not warrant a second glance, he thought.

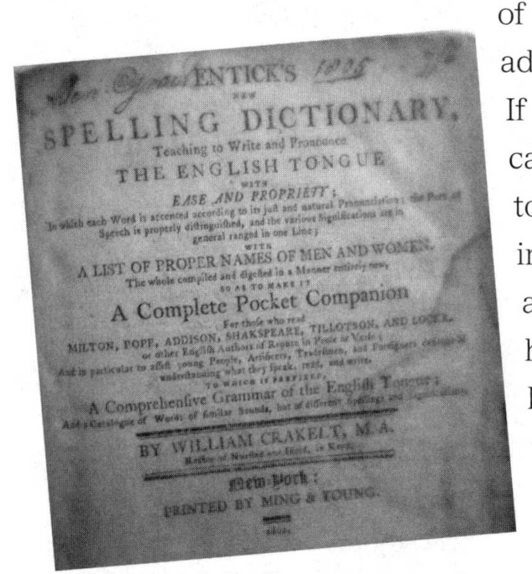

ENTICK'S
NEW
SPELLING DICTIONARY,
Teaching to Write and Pronounce
THE ENGLISH TONGUE
WITH
EASE AND PROPRIETY;
In which each Word is accented according to its just and natural Pronunciation; [illegible]
Speech is properly distinguished, and the various Significations are in
general ranged in one Line;
WITH
A LIST OF PROPER NAMES OF MEN AND WOMEN.
The whole compiled and digested in a Manner entirely new,
SO AS TO MAKE IT
A Complete Pocket Companion
For those who read
MILTON, POPE, ADDISON, SHAKSPEARE, TILLOTSON, AND LOCKE,
or other English Authors of Repute in Prose or Verse;
And in particular to assist young People, Artificers, Tradesmen, and Foreigners [illegible]
understanding what they speak, read, and write.
TO WHICH IS PREFIXED,
A Comprehensive Grammar of the English Tongue;
And a Catalogue of Words of similar Sounds, but of different [illegible]
BY WILLIAM CRAKELT, M. A.
[illegible]
New-York:
PRINTED BY MING & YOUNG.
[illegible]

The Culper Ring used a pocket dictionary like this one to create one of their codes.

With Rivington's print shop operating just down the street,

and as someone who enjoyed an established relationship with the owner, Townsend had no shortage of books available for sending messages the way Washington suggested. But Townsend, using his invisible ink, seems to have preferred an alternative means of his own design: when the courier (usually Woodhull or Roe, judging from his store's ledger) arrived to pick up the goods he had purchased to bring back to Long Island, among them would be a packet of blank writing paper. Concealed within those loose sheets of paper was a seemingly blank one that contained the invisible letter, to be rendered readable once it reached its destination and the stain was applied. All in all, this method worked extremely well as an innocuous way to smuggle reports out of the city.

Various mastheads from the papers James Rivington published.

With these new security measures in place, and Culper Junior and Agent 355 firmly established in their roles in New York, the ring could now begin to forward intelligence more swiftly, more safely, and in greater detail than before, though the risk of detection and capture remained. The life of a spy always requires looking over one's shoulder, but now Washington's operatives could enjoy at least a little more freedom to speak about their observances, with less need to censor their words in case a letter fell into the wrong hands.

The added security was just in time, too. Suspicions and tensions were beginning to rise as the summer of 1779 reached its peak, and all the agents were feeling the stress. Indeed, letters were now being searched by the British with regularity as they left the city. Jonas Hawkins twice believed he was in danger of being found out and destroyed the messages he was carrying from Townsend.

In addition to British searches, the couriers also faced dangers from increasingly active privateers working for the British. These privateers were authorized to board and search any boat they felt was suspicious. In his letter dated November 1, 1779, Tallmadge wrote to General Washington of the growing hazards faced by the once-fearless Caleb Brewster: "The boat that crosses for dispatches from C—— has been chased quite across the Sound by those plunderers, perhaps for the sake of being the more secret in their Villany, while our crew has suspected them to be the Enemy. Indeed if some stop cannot be put to such nefarious practices C—— will not risque, nor 725 [Brewster] go over for dispatches."

CHAPTER 26

Thwarting a Plot

Meanwhile, there was a covert storm brewing in New York—one that Townsend was in the process of uncovering and confirming—that threatened the Americans not through bloodshed or siege but through their pocketbooks.

Although the colonists used British currency for buying and selling, they also used paper money printed by the colonial governments. These bills were not backed by gold or silver and so were not worth much. To make them worthwhile, both the buyer and the seller had to believe the money exchange was fair. The British, recognizing how fragile the American currency was, decided to weaken it further by running counterfeiting operations aboard British ships and even onshore where possible. They printed fake colonial money and used it to pay merchants. The operation introduced thousands of fake bills into the economy, so every bill was now worth even less than before.

The Continental Congress had made some efforts to combat the

The colonies did not have metal to make coins so they issued paper money. This is a four-dollar bill issued by the United Colonies in 1776.

counterfeiting but had limited success. Eventually, they developed a special paper, of a very precise quality and thickness, that would be used to produce the bulk of the money minted in Philadelphia for the colonies—a paper they hoped would be extremely difficult to replicate. This would allow the government much greater control over the amount of bills in circulation.

Townsend learned of a British plot to steal the paper. On November 27, 1779, he wrote with urgency to Washington that "several reams of the paper made for the last emissions struck by Congress have been procured from Philadelphia." The safeguard that the Americans were counting on to protect their currency had been breached. Somehow, whether through negligence or a double agent, the paper and possibly even the printer plates had made their way to New York, where the British would use them to churn out perfect counterfeits. Distribution of the fakes in New York would drive down prices and sink the economy of the colonies right in the heart of their main trading hub.

The magnitude of this plot and the fact that the worthless bills would be undetectable before it was too late made this intelligence of utmost importance. With word from the Culpers delivered swiftly, Washington was able to alert Congress to the scheme. The resulting action—a cancellation of all colonial bills a few months later, in March 1780—was drastic and potentially devastating in itself, but far less destructive to the American economy and morale than a sneak attack on its currency would have been.

Just how had Townsend uncovered such a plan? He may have happened upon some gossip by lucky coincidence, but the certainty with which Townsend outlined the plan for Tallmadge and Washington indicates that he had a much more intimate knowledge of the scheme than just hearsay. His likely source? The newest member of the ring: newspaper editor and former Loyalist James Rivington.

Sometime in 1779, Rivington secretly threw in his lot with the Americans and began to work alongside Robert Townsend gathering

A twenty-dollar bill issued in 1775. A colonial bill was known as a "continental."

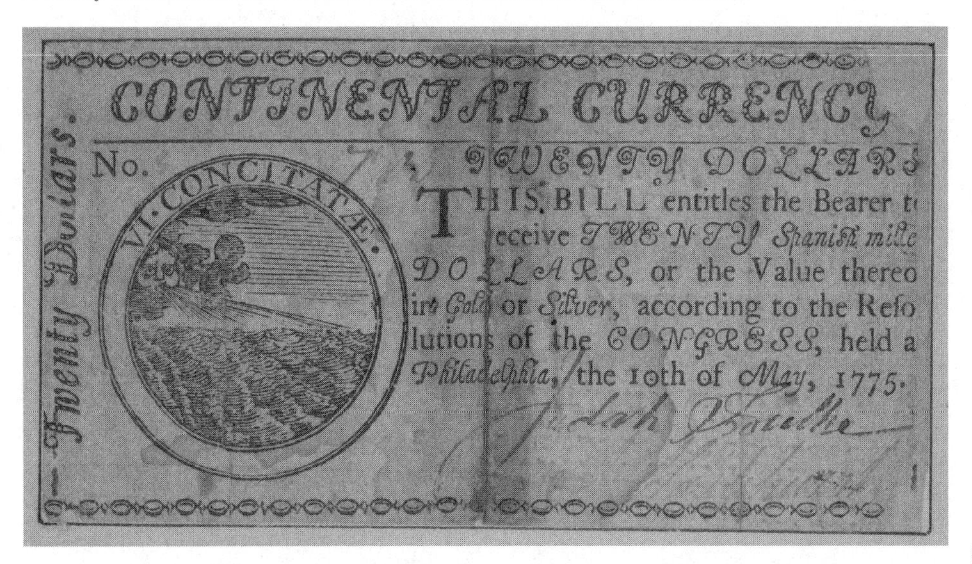

information. Rivington proved a valuable asset to Townsend's work. Taking advantage of his profession, he provided books for the spies' use. Sometimes the book bindings hid slips of paper holding intelligence that Rivington himself had gleaned from the Loyalist guests and friends who patronized his coffeehouse.

The British were being played, and from the least likely of corners. But they remained oblivious to the double-dealings in their midst. In the coffeehouse, British officers, surrounded by their admirers, discussed their plans. They were relaxed and confident. And they were being carefully watched and listened to all the while.

Now Washington had tasted victory; his agents had outsmarted the enemy in their own territory. It could be done. By revealing the counterfeiting plot, the Culper Ring had proved that New York was not some insurmountable fortress; they had penetrated its vault of secrets successfully and unmasked an entire plot before it could be played out to its catastrophic end. Best of all, the enemy had no way of knowing at what stage the plan might have been leaked, and no way of tracing back any breaches of secrecy. Washington's informants, therefore, were relatively safe from detection and could continue their activities without too much concern for their welfare.

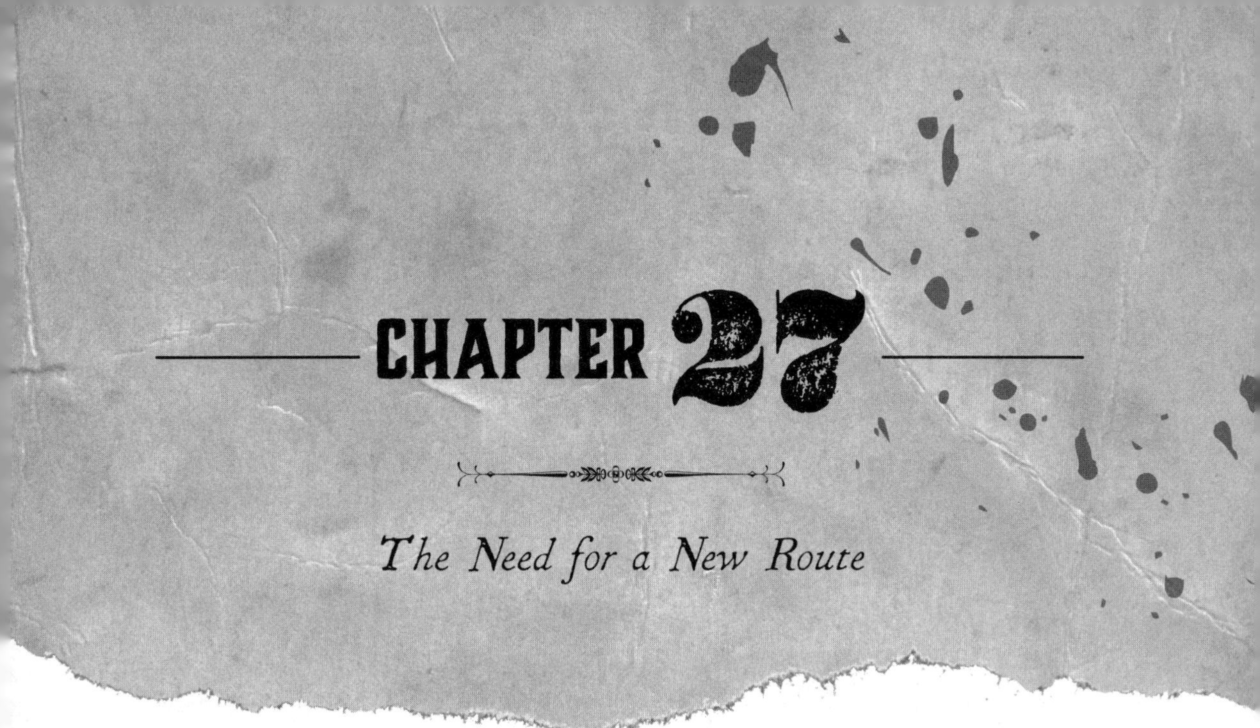

CHAPTER 27

The Need for a New Route

Washington was certain there were many more plots afoot. Now that one plan had been foiled, another would soon be hatched—probably with more speed this time, to minimize the risk of leaks. But the smuggled messages were not meeting the pressing demands Washington was facing. Events were accelerating rapidly, and the laborious means of conveying the letters out of occupied New York and Long Island, into Connecticut, and overland to Washington's camp was too slow. Instead of offering new information, the Culper Ring's intelligence was now providing verification of facts the general had already learned. He pored over the maps as he would before a battle; perhaps there was a way to convey messages across the Hudson River or via Staten Island? He wrote as much to Tallmadge, urging him to talk to Culper Senior about such an option, hoping to impress upon the ring the importance of timely reports.

Washington felt a growing sense of urgency about seeing the

cracks in New York's armor pursued even more aggressively. If the British were plotting any offensive maneuvers from the city, he wanted to be prepared.

Townsend looked for new couriers who could carry messages northward across the Hudson, as the general had requested, instead of across the Sound and through Connecticut. Rather than choose an outsider, he turned to a family member, a cousin named James Townsend, who was only sixteen or seventeen years old at the time. The young man had no idea as to the exact nature of the letters with which he was entrusted; he only knew that they contained sensitive information that was important to his grave, somber cousin—and that the letters would land him in prison if his mission was found out.

James set off under the assumed identity of a Loyalist visiting relatives outside the city. His travels progressed smoothly until he stopped at the home of the Deausenberry family, who were secretly Patriots in an otherwise Loyalist-dominated area. James seems to have played his part so convincingly that the Deausenberry daughters, young women about his own age, believed his cover story and suspected that he might even be a Loyalist spy. In the hope of causing him to spill his story, they pretended to be Loyalists, too. The boy set about to convince the family he was harmless, telling completely false tales of how he had helped the British. As the daughters complimented him, he told even taller tales. Finally, the girls' elder brother, John Deausenberry, leaped from a hiding place and declared that James was a prisoner.

A terrified James was immediately carted off to the American army camp nearby, where he was searched thoroughly, and John

Deausenberry gave a detailed deposition on the matter. To the great disappointment of both the Deausenberrys and the soldiers, nothing of interest was found on James, though they did commandeer the two sheets of paper he was carrying, which contained a groan-worthy poem called "The Lady's Dress" on a page folded in a peculiar manner, signed with a nearly illegible "S.T." The soldiers sent the letters on to headquarters, and James was held in Patriot custody.

Poor James's mission was not a complete debacle, because the papers did reach Washington. He recognized the unusual manner of folding (his own suggestion from a letter of September 24, 1779) and knew the initials "S.T." indicated that stain was to be applied. The handwriting, too, was a giveaway that the papers had come from none other than Culper Junior.

Washington was furious that so much unnecessary attention had been drawn to covert operations, wasting resources, and he had to intervene personally to get James released, since his captors continued to believe he was a British spy. Tallmadge was briefed on the situation, and he, in turn, made sure that Woodhull understood the depth of Washington's displeasure.

Part Three

CHAPTER 28

The French Arrive

In June 1780, a fleet of French ships was crossing the Atlantic, coming to give the Americans a much-needed boost of men, might, and morale. If the British intercepted them, it would be devastating for the Patriot cause.

Washington had received intelligence that the fleet would be arriving soon at Newport, Rhode Island. But he could not be sure whether the British knew the same thing or had only rumors and suspicions from which to operate. If the British were ignorant of the specifics, the Americans might have the element of surprise on their side. If the British had advance knowledge, they could move troops to engage the French as soon as they disembarked, or even prevent their landing in the first place. It had taken a long time to win over the French, and the Americans could not afford to squander their new ally's good favor.

On July 10, the French fleet dropped anchor at Narragansett

Bay, Rhode Island. Washington sent an urgent letter to Tallmadge. Tallmadge received the letter on July 14 and immediately replied to the general that he would set out the next morning to find Brewster. Once located, Brewster eagerly set off to find Woodhull, who, unfortunately, was ill with a fever and could not travel. Instead, Austin Roe leaped upon a horse and headed straight for New York to alert Townsend, an exhausting fifty-five-mile trip one way. Washington knew by now that General Clinton would be aware of the landing, too. Townsend's mission was to spy out the British response to the fleet's arrival.

Roe waited in Manhattan four days while Townsend (and very likely Agent 355) made inquiries and gathered as much information as possible from their acquaintances among the British officers. There was indeed movement of British troops and ships; they were preparing for something. Townsend recorded the findings in invisible ink between the lines of an order form for goods from his store, and included a fake note apologizing that the merchandise was not available at the time but would be forwarded when it arrived. Roe carried the note back with him—a simple cover story as to why he was carrying papers but no merchandise, in case he should be searched—and gave the sensitive letter to Woodhull. Woodhull passed it on to Brewster that same night to row across the Sound, adding pressing directions: "The enclosed requires your immediate departure this day by all means let not an hour pass: for this day must not be lost. You have news of the greatest consequence perhaps that ever happened to your country."

Brewster rushed the letter straight to Washington's headquarters. Alexander Hamilton, Washington's closest aide, received the report on the afternoon of July 21.

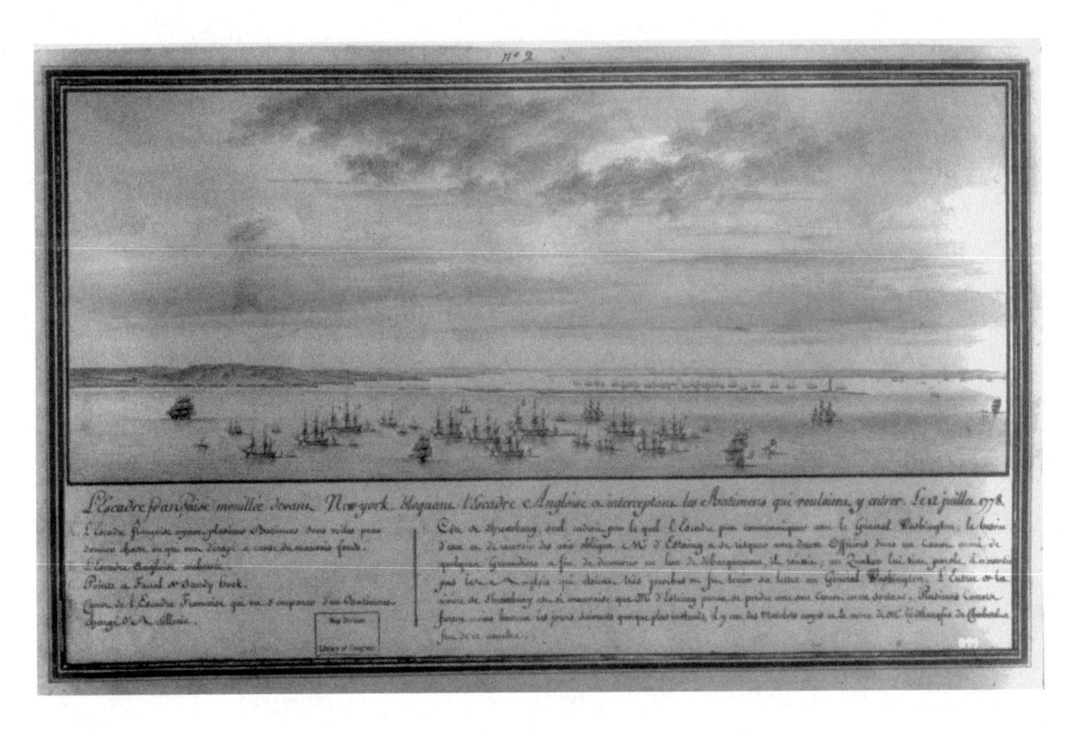

The French were already helping the Patriots even before the fleet arrived in 1780.

CHAPTER 29

Washington's Gamble

Washington carefully considered the possibilities. He desperately wanted to capture New York City, and with Clinton leading most of the British troops stationed there northward toward Newport, Rhode Island, to engage the French, this could be his best opportunity. But Washington also knew better than to act rashly. He called together several of his top officers, and they discussed the likelihood of a successful attack on New York; the prevailing sentiment was that it would be unwise. Even with Clinton and a large number of his men gone, the city was still well fortified, and the battle would most likely end as a siege lasting many days, giving Clinton time to return with his soldiers and engage the Americans. Regretfully, Washington yielded to his counselors and agreed to reject his ambitions to recapture the city, but the brilliant strategist realized he could still capitalize on Manhattan's vulnerability.

Satisfied with the decision not to attack New York, Washington dismissed his officers—and then hurriedly began drawing up plans and penning correspondence signaling that a full-fledged attack upon Manhattan would occur as soon as Clinton's forces were clear of the city and too near to Newport to be easily recalled. The parcel was dispatched with a courier who hastily left camp with very specific instructions on where and when to "deliver" the documents. Then Washington waited.

A few hours later, the man stumbled up to a British outpost with the bundle of papers. He told the soldiers he had found it lying by the side of the road, assuming it had tumbled out of the poorly secured saddlebags of a rider traveling at breakneck speed. How it got there wasn't important, the British immediately concluded. A quick glance revealed battle plans for a pending attack on New York and letters

French vessels readying to return to Newport, Rhode Island.

outlining the strategy, all coming from the hand of Washington himself. The soldiers roused their senior officers, who quickly decided that Clinton and his troops must be recalled. Defeating the newly arrived French troops was important, but holding New York was doubly so.

The British ships did an about-face to sail back to New York Harbor, where Clinton ordered his troops to brace the city for an attack that could come at any time. The whole city held its breath, every citizen straining to hear the first sound of cannon fire breaking the silence as the Americans advanced.

They waited. And while they waited, the French disembarked and moved to an area of safety to await their marching orders, with no naval attacks upon their ships and no ground offensive from Clinton's army.

Washington's gamble—made possible by the Culper Ring information—had paid off beautifully. The victory was bittersweet, though, because his first choice would have been to recapture New York. But he had been able to secure the safe arrival of the French reinforcements by planting information about a fake attack.

The quality of the Culper Ring's information, and the care they exercised in delivering it, had enabled him to both understand the plans of the British and arrive at the decision not to risk an attack on New York. The ring had more than proved its worth, but the war was not yet won.

CHAPTER 30

The Most Powerful Man on the Hudson River: Benedict Arnold

Now that the city of New York seemed to be secure, General Clinton became interested in expanding his grasp on New York beyond the boundaries of Long Island and Manhattan, and was eyeing the Hudson Valley as a means of controlling the land along the Hudson River as well as the harbor at its mouth.

At the same time, an American general named Benedict Arnold heard that the command at Fort West Point was available and decided it seemed the perfect solution to his various woes. Arnold had been living the high life in Philadelphia, but recent unpleasantness had wounded his ego, and he had found himself in an all-too-familiar position: humiliated, angry, and desperate to prove his worth. He was about to show the world just how important he really was. If the Americans couldn't see his value, the British would.

Arnold had been involved in a number of key American victories and had distinguished himself as an insightful strategist and able

Portrait of Benedict Arnold by American artist John Trumbull.

officer. But his talents were not nearly so celebrated as Arnold believed was his due. He had also been involved in somewhat shady business. An audit of the records of the 1775 invasion of Quebec that he helped lead showed a substantial sum tied to Arnold for which there was no accounting or receipts; according to practice, the amount due was his own responsibility. He now owed the Continental Army more than a thousand pounds!

Arnold and his wife, the daughter of Loyalists, mingled with the British troops at parties in her parents' home. Arnold met Major André there and began to hatch a plan to trade his loyalty for cash.

While he may not have relished the thought of moving from cosmopolitan Philadelphia to remote West Point, the idea of being in absolute authority in his own fort must have appealed to his pride. He could quit the city, assume control of the strategic fort, and at precisely the right time turn it over to the British. He would then collect his reward, pay off his debts, and enjoy a life of leisure as a man who had made the king's victory over the rebellion possible.

In New York, General Clinton, too, recognized the potential of Fort West Point; it was situated fifty-five miles north of Manhattan, on a sharp turn of the Hudson River. From there, it was possible to control the access of ships to the rest of the river, thereby limiting or opening the movement of troops, supplies, and goods for trade. It was, in many ways, the key to the rest of the state. Through Major André, he urged Arnold to press his case for the command of the fort.

At the end of July, with the French troops safely disembarked in Rhode Island, Washington prepared to ride out to meet them and proposed that Arnold lead a raid against some of Clinton's troops stationed around New York at the same time. Arnold pleaded to be excused from such exertion, saying that an injury had left him with a stiff ankle, and his doctors had recommended that he not take command of an army until it healed. Conceding to Arnold's requests and complaints, Washington kept him off the battlefield and diverted him instead to the less physically demanding post as commander of West Point, exactly as Arnold had hoped. On August 3, 1780, Benedict

The fort at West Point on a turn in the Hudson River. This engraving was created in 1780 by James Smillie.

Arnold found himself the most powerful man on the Hudson.

He wasted no time in making the most of his new position. He began repairing the fort and stocking it with as many provisions as possible. If he was going to turn West Point over to the British, he might as well win points with his new commanders by outfitting it at the Americans' expense.

Even more urgently, Arnold began to inquire about the names and addresses of Patriot spies he claimed might be of importance to him in defending the fort against any planned attacks by the British. Of particular interest to Arnold was the ring operating in New York, upon whom Washington had relied so heavily both in the recent incident with the French fleet and in previous matters of significant intelligence, such as troop movements on Long Island and the foiled counterfeiting plan. The commander in chief declined the request out of both honor and necessity; he purposely did not know the identity of most of his spies, and he had sworn to uphold the secrecy of those he did know.

By September, Arnold needed only a few details taken care of to bring his whole plan to fruition. First, he needed an opportunity to familiarize the British with the plans of the fort so that they could exploit its vulnerabilities and storm it as swiftly as possible. Second, he needed time to get the necessary British men and weapons hidden in place, to ensure that any resistance the Patriots offered would be futile.

He sent a letter to an American outpost, informing them that a certain merchant from the city by the name of John Anderson might be passing their way and begging their assistance in securing him safe passage to West Point. Then Arnold tried to arrange a meeting with André outside the city to finalize their negotiations and plans for handing over the fort.

When the long-anticipated meeting finally took place, André was to pose as the prosperous businessman.

CHAPTER 31

What Robert Townsend Saw

Townsend, meanwhile, found that when he left his shop to observe the goings-on around Manhattan that September, he could not help but notice the uptick in preparations along the docks. The British were clearly fitting ships for some kind of engagement, though Townsend could not be sure if this was merely a response to the arrival of the French fleet and the fear that a naval battle might be brewing, or if it was with some other specific aim. Even the soldiers and sailors with whom he conversed were uncertain as to their orders. It seemed unlikely that significant troop movements would be following so closely on the heels of the misinformation regarding Washington's supposed plans to attack the city and the unanticipated recall of troops. Then again, the blow to Clinton's pride that incident had delivered might have prompted him to plan an aggressive response, simply to prove he would not be made the fool.

None of the spies knew, however, quite what they were in the midst of in September 1780. The reports from the city, the strange behaviors, and the activity with the ships—Tallmadge couldn't quite put his finger on it, but his instincts told him something was not right. He felt as if he had nearly all the elements in front of him, almost all the clues gathered, but he was not sure what he was looking at, nor what the picture was that he needed to assemble. That he had letters on his desk from his merchant spy in New York regarding an officer from the city venturing toward West Point seemed wholly unconnected. Despite all the hints he received from Agent 355, Woodhull, and Townsend, Tallmadge didn't connect the dots until it was almost too late.

CHAPTER 32

Benjamin Tallmadge Figures It Out

Two meetings were set up between Arnold and André in his disguise as John Anderson. Neither worked out. Eventually, André boarded a British ship moored near West Point. He was rowed ashore, and he finally met Arnold to discuss the handover. During the meeting, the ship set sail for the south, so André/Anderson had to travel back through Patriot-held territory to British-held Manhattan by horse.

On September 23, André was stopped along the road by three eagle-eyed Patriot militiamen. André produced a letter of safe passage signed by General Arnold, but that didn't satisfy the scouts. They searched his person and found that he had papers hidden in his socks.

The papers, including letters between Anderson and Arnold and what looked like plans of a fort, were sent to General Washington, but the prisoner was released on orders of Colonel Jameson, who was in charge of the area, and escorted back to Arnold at West Point.

At Washington's headquarters, Tallmadge heard talk of the newly apprehended prisoner named John Anderson; something seemed strange about the story, but so much had of late that it was hard to pinpoint what was so unsettling. As Tallmadge sat reviewing the letters at his desk, he happened to spot a note from General Arnold sent some days previously, informing him of a certain man named John Anderson who might pass Tallmadge's way: "I have to request that you will give him an escort of two Horse to bring him on his way to this place, and send an express to me that I may meet him." Suddenly, it all made sense: the prisoner, the strange reports he was

A painting by John McNevin imagines a secret nighttime meeting between André and Arnold.

This imagined scene shows Benedict Arnold convincing John André to hide papers in his boot. The picture by Charles Blauvelt was published in 1874.

receiving from the Culpers in New York, and Arnold's odd request.

Hearing a full account of the story from the colonel who had released André, Tallmadge put the bits of information together and concluded that a major betrayal was at hand.

Tallmadge persuaded Jameson to rescind his order and bring André back to the army camp just north of White Plains, New York, while they awaited word from Washington. Oddly enough, Jameson still insisted on informing Arnold of the turn of events. "Strange as it may seem," Tallmadge wrote, "Lt. Col. J. would persist in his purpose of sending his letter to Gen. Arnold—The letter did go on, and was the first information that Arch Traitor received that his plot was blown up. The Officer returned [to Jameson's camp] with his prisoner early the next morning."

Jameson's decision to alert Arnold to the matter, while shocking in retrospect, was quite understandable at the time, given Arnold's reputation. For one thing, Arnold was widely trusted by many officers of the Continental Army. He was also widely feared, and Jameson was willing to take extreme steps to protect himself from the man's wrath for not following his directives. Had Tallmadge not been as acutely attuned to subtle clues and not been actively trying to piece together the Culper Ring's reports, he, too, might have fallen under Arnold's spell and failed to realize who John Anderson really was.

Even now, Tallmadge kept the spies in mind and realized that more than just the fate of Fort West Point was at stake. The surrender of the fort had to be stopped at all costs, but in a somewhat delicate way. André would not have broadcast his travel plans beyond a select circle, and the collapse of his plan could endanger the spies who had helped unravel the plot. If word reached the British that there was a mole in André's inner circle, Agent 355 and any of her known associates—like Townsend—could be quickly unmasked. The entire ring would collapse, and the gallows would become a little more crowded. Tallmadge would have to act swiftly but carefully.

CHAPTER 33

The Turncoat Escapes

General Washington and Alexander Hamilton were riding toward Fort West Point on the evening of Sunday, September 24. They had been visiting Hartford, Connecticut. Washington anticipated that Arnold would be happy to see him, just as he was eager to see what improvements Arnold had put into effect at the fort, now that he had been in command nearly two months.

Arnold knew that Washington was on his way. Just after the first of Washington's entourage arrived, so did the letter from Colonel Jameson explaining that a gentleman by the name of Anderson, carrying passes issued by Arnold, had been captured and was in confinement while some odd papers and plans found on him were sent to General Washington via an express rider. It was all a wicked plan by the British, Jameson concluded, to besmirch Benedict Arnold's good name and to cause division in the ranks by undermining the Continental Army's confidence in him. He

Benedict Arnold escapes to the Vulture.

felt Arnold should be made aware of the slanderous efforts being made against him by the enemy.

The jig was up. Arnold's worst fears had all been realized: the Americans were aware (or soon would be) of the depth of his treachery, but the British had yet to do anything to capture the fort and, without the plans, likely never would be able to do so. Thus, he was a traitor to one group, and hardly the hero he had anticipated becoming to the other. Now, he would be nothing more than a failed turncoat—if he were even able to escape with his life, that is.

Arnold dashed off toward the water, telling his staff that he would return promptly, just as soon as he sorted out some urgent matter across the river. He called for his bargemen to row him as swiftly as possible downstream, toward where HMS *Vulture* had recently retreated, explaining to the confused men at the oars that they would receive two gallons of rum apiece if they did their job quickly, as he would need to turn around very shortly to meet General Washington for his much-anticipated visit. They exerted themselves admirably. The barge reached the *Vulture* under a flag of truce, which kept them from being fired upon and allowed Arnold to board in safety. His loyal crew were also taken aboard, where Arnold promptly informed them that they were now prisoners of the British army.

Safely tucked away on a ship in New York, Benedict Arnold was now enjoying the luxuries of high living, including the knowledge that his wife and infant son were safe from retribution: he wrote to Washington asking if the general would guarantee their secure passage to him, and Washington agreed, not believing it proper to punish a child for the sins of his father. With Arnold's true loyalties now exposed and his body, mind, and energies openly aligned with the British, he could pose no further threat to American forts or forces under his command.

But Arnold was not finished sowing chaos for the Culper Ring. As Tallmadge had feared, his capture spelled danger for the secret six.

CHAPTER 34

The Prisoner Is Executed

Arnold's backhanded, cowardly character contrasted sharply with that of his co-conspirator, André, who comported himself with dignity by all accounts, and treated his captors with respect and even friendliness.

But this was wartime, and there must be winners and losers. André had been caught and captured at the same game that Tallmadge was playing; they both knew the rules, the rewards, the risks—and they both knew the penalties.

Major André is captured. This image is by the famous American lithographers Nathaniel Currier and James Merritt Ives.

In the tense days that followed, a prisoner

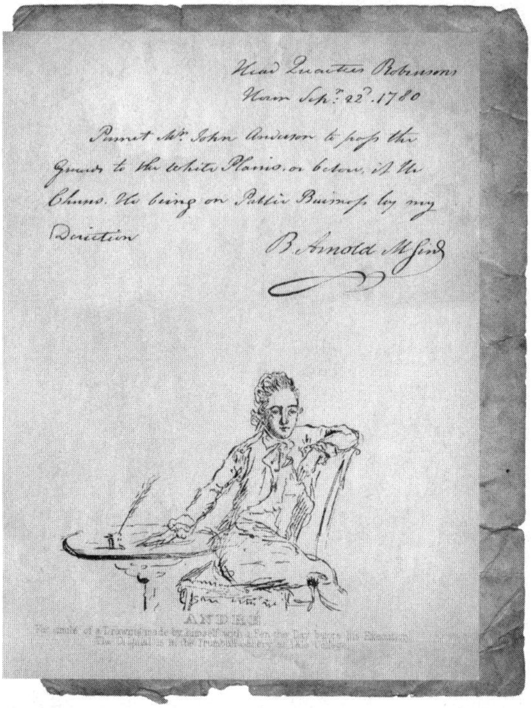

exchange was proposed, as was often the case when high-ranking officers were captured. General Washington was agreeable only if the prisoner surrendered was Arnold; General Clinton would not agree to these terms, so Washington proceeded as he would with any common spy. Washington granted André a trial, in which several of the top officers among the Continental Army and her allies were speedily assembled to hear arguments. André maintained that because he had been trapped and captured behind enemy lines, he was technically not a spy scouting the territory in the uniform of his service but was, instead, a prisoner of war. All such prisoners, he reasoned, can be expected to at least consider making an escape dressed in civilian clothes. The plea failed to persuade the tribunal. André was sentenced to death by hanging on September 29.

John André drew this self-portrait on the day before he was hanged. It is at the bottom of a letter written by Benedict Arnold.

The sentence was to be carried out on October 2, just over a week after André's capture. He carried himself with dignity and propriety, stoically recognizing his sad fate as simply one of the unfortunate dangers of war.

A blindfolded André is put to death by hanging.

CHAPTER 35

The Ring in Peril

Even though Arnold was exposed, the plot to surrender Fort West Point was shattered, and André was dead, the danger to the Culper Ring was still very much alive. "I am happy to think that Arnold does not know my name," Townsend noted in a letter to Tallmadge. Clearly, Townsend was anticipating what all of the covert operatives must have been dreading: that Arnold would disclose the identities of any spies known to him in order to keep himself in the good graces of the British.

Woodhull sent a letter, dated October 26, in which he explained to Tallmadge and Washington, "I have this day returned from New York, and am sorry to informe you that the present commotions and watchfullness of the Enemy at New York hath resolved C. Jur. for the present time to quit writing and retire into the country for a time.—Most certainly the enemy are very severe, and the spirits of our friends very low."

Just as the confusion of the Arnold betrayal began to dissipate, a blow was struck that threw all covert agents into a state of fear once again.

Woodhull wrote to Tallmadge, on November 12, of some disturbing news: "Several of our dear friends were imprisoned, in particular one that hath been ever serviceable to this correspondence. This step so dejected the spirits of C. Junr. that he resolved to leave New York for a time." The letter goes on to add that Austin Roe had returned from New York and that Brewster had narrowly escaped capture while crossing the Sound. There is no indication that Rivington was ever suspected or that his newspaper operations were suspended, and the ring's satellite members who had functioned as couriers all seemed to be safe. The person imprisoned enjoyed very close ties to Townsend, making it likely that the "ever serviceable" friend apprehended was none other than Agent 355. Whether she was found out and betrayed by Arnold or caught because of general suspicion, the lady's capture shattered the morale of the other five spies.

Townsend's spying activities largely ceased during the season of his withdrawal from business. Washington took advantage of the time to shift his focus temporarily from Manhattan to the surrounding areas. Thanks in part to the reports still coming in from Woodhull on Long Island, Washington began to reconsider Tallmadge's earlier proposals to storm certain vulnerable locations on Long Island.

On November 21, 1780, Tallmadge (now a colonel in the Continental Army) led a contingent of eighty men selected from his Second Dragoons—along with Caleb Brewster, who is listed as a captain in the operation—from Fairfield, Connecticut, across Long Island Sound in whaleboats, to the town of Mount Sinai, roughly six miles from Tallmadge's native Setauket. Battling rain and high winds, they marched roughly twenty miles through the night of November 22, straight across the island to Mastic on the southern shore, and attacked Fort St. George on the morning of November 23. Constructed and fortified the previous year by staunch Loyalists and named for the patron saint of England, the fort had a large stockpile of supplies and provisions, including an ample amount of hay upon which British soldiers in the area depended to feed their livestock. After a brief fight against the well-armed residents, Tallmadge's men were able to seize control, destroy the stockpile, burn the hay, and take the fort's inhabitants prisoner—all while suffering only one injury on their side. The prisoners were marched back across the island to the boats that were waiting under guard, and the whole company crossed the Sound again for Connecticut.

Washington was pleased by the efforts and applauded Tallmadge in a personal letter. Woodhull, too, sent his congratulations, writing on November 28, "The burning the forage is agreeable to me and must hurt the enemy much."

It was not a major battle from a strategic standpoint, but it delivered an important morale boost to the Patriots and provided a psychological victory over the British by proving that New York and Long Island had not been forgotten, nor were they invincible.

Part Four

CHAPTER 36

Closing in on the Ring

The Culper Ring stayed busy (if not active in spying) as the calendar turned from 1780 to 1781. Late in the winter, Caleb Brewster captured a British boat and took eight prisoners, including two officers. Townsend resumed his business and reopened his shop in the city in March; Woodhull tried to persuade him to start gathering intelligence again. Townsend believed that the British had dispatched a spy of their own in New York who was actively trying to root out the sources and paths of the Culpers' information, and he insisted on lying low. The matter was dropped until the end of April, when Tallmadge could finally report the pending resurrection of the ring's activities, with a few adjustments made to their former routine. "The plan which he [Woodhull] has consented to adopt, on certain conditions, is for him to remain for the most part on Long Island and C. Junr. whom he thinks might be engaged again, to reside constantly at New York," he wrote to Washington on the twenty-fifth. "That some confidential person must of course be employed to carry dispatches as it would cause suspicions which might lead to detection if either of the Culpers should be frequently passing from New York to Setauket, &c. they being men of some considerable note."

Washington preferred a more timely delivery of intelligence, but he agreed to this arrangement. The Culpers' reports were essential to the continued success of the Americans, even if they did take a few days longer to arrive.

However, Townsend adamantly refused to put pen to paper. He had seen how André had been done in by the discovery of papers and plans, hard evidence he could neither deny nor talk his way out of. He would be happy to convey orally whatever information he had observed, Townsend explained to Woodhull when they met in the city in early May, but the risk of trying to smuggle written documents out of Manhattan was far too great.

CHAPTER 37

Rivington Delivers Yorktown

General Washington remained hopeful that the next major military engagement would be focused on retaking New York, but he was depending heavily on the French navy, which was currently in the Caribbean; the success of the mission would rely in large part upon the men, supplies, and ships that the French could provide to support the inadequately manned and provisioned American forces. When word reached the general that the fleet would be sailing in August 1781 to Yorktown, Virginia, and not to New York, he was disappointed but knew he could not afford to squander such an opportunity.

Hoping to confuse General Clinton, he left 2,500 men north of New York and arranged for a fake invasion of Staten Island. Then he set out on a hot summer march to Virginia. Because the British had ample warships and the Patriots had none of their own, Washington longed for intelligence about the codes the British used to communicate among their ships so he could determine their orders in advance and inform the French.

Whether someone had left a copy in Rivington's coffeehouse or the British had commissioned him to print more is not clear, but somehow he managed to procure the entire British naval codebook. Rivington passed it on to Allen McLane, an independent intelligence agent.

Both McLane and the codebook made it safely down to Virginia by the end of the summer, and Washington was able to transport the book to the French admiral by mid-September. In French hands, it was a more effective resource than the Americans could have dared hope for, and its loss was more devastating than the British could have imagined.

American, British, and Hessian soldiers in close contact in Yorktown.

CHAPTER 38

The Beginning of the End for the British

The siege of Yorktown was a roaring success for the Patriots, thanks in no small part to the codebook, which allowed the French to anticipate nearly every movement of the British fleet. Despite his continued assurances that he would send reinforcements to Virginia, General Clinton failed to deliver, paralyzed by the fear of leaving New York vulnerable to attack. Trapped by both land and sea, the British general in Virginia, Lieutenant General Charles Cornwallis, was unable to muster the power to break through in either direction. He could not attack; he could not retreat. A white flag was the only option. He surrendered on October 19.

To military leaders on both sides, the events at Yorktown made it clear that the conflict was reaching its natural end. The Americans had stood their ground and doggedly fought for every inch of land they deemed rightfully their own; the British government was finally recognizing that superior military muscle was not enough to make the determined Patriot army back down, especially when they had powerful allies on their side. On March 28, 1782, word reached New York from London that the House of Commons had voted to end all offensive strikes in the American colonies.

Loyalists in the remaining British strongholds of New York; Savannah, Georgia; and Charleston, South Carolina, who had been certain of coming out of the war on the winning side, felt betrayed by the Crown. Facing an uncertain future, they began to make plans: should they stay and rebuild their lives, or should they emigrate back to Europe or northward to British Canada?

The majority of Loyalists, like the majority of Patriots, were humble men and women of modest means: small landowners, tenant farmers, laborers in the cities, fishermen and longshoremen along the coasts, hunters and traders in the frontiers of the Appalachian Mountains. In deciding where to live out the remainder of their days, they had to take into consideration the inclinations of their neighbors and their own consciences; it would not be a pleasant thing to be forever regarded as "the neighbor who fought against our government." Some of the wealthiest citizens had already booked passage back to England; now the common folk began to do the same.

General Charles O'Hara, representing General Cornwallis, surrenders his sword to Comte de Rochambeau. George Washington stands next to the French general.

CHAPTER 39

Townsend's Last Letter

Townsend had firmly declined to commit anything to writing back in May. But during the long summer, he could see the shaky position of the city and knew that Washington needed the best intelligence he could offer in order to calculate the next—and maybe final—move of the war. Townsend shouldered the responsibility of delivering the latest report himself, figuring that if he was arrested and tried as a spy, he would have only himself to blame.

The message Townsend delivered to Tallmadge, with the date September 19, 1782, written across the top, is the final surviving letter from Culper Junior's hand. The news painted a city in upheaval:

> The last packet, so far from bringing better news to the loyalists, has indeed brought the clearest and unequivocal Proofs that the independence of America is unconditionally

to be acknowledged, nor will there be any conditions insisted on for those who joined the King's Standard.

It is said that an Expedition is now forming at N.Y. and by many conjectured to be against the French Fleet &c. at Boston; a number of British Troops were embarking when I left the city on the 14th and 15th inst[ant]. But I conversed fully with one of Carleton's Aides on this subject, who told me that I might depend they were bound to the W. Indies or Halifax. For my own part I have no expectation that they think of any offensive movements. The above gentleman, with whom I am most intimately connected, informed me that it is now under consideration to send all the B. Troops to the West Indies.

. . . Sir Guy himself says that he thinks it not improbable that the next Packet may bring orders for an evacuation of N. York.

A fleet is getting ready to sail for the Bay of Fundy about the first of October to transport a large number of Refugees to that Quarter. The Aide above referred to informs us that he thinks it probable he shall go there himself. Indeed, I never saw such general distress and dissatisfaction in my life as is painted in the countenance of every Tory at N.Y.

The Beef Contractors had orders a few days past to cease purchasing any more for the Navy and from the appearance of things the whole fleet are getting ready for a movement.

I am myself uncertain when the Troops will leave N.Y. but

> I must confess I rather believe if the King's Magazines can be removed, that they will leave us this fall.

Townsend's prediction of a British evacuation before the end of 1782 proved a little too optimistic. Finally, on February 3, 1783, the government of Great Britain formally acknowledged what were once its American colonies as the independent United States of America.

THE LAST BOAT-LOAD OF THE BRITISH LEAVING NEW YORK.

EVACUATION OF NEW YORK BY THE BRITISH, 1783.

OUR Revolutionary centennials, which opened with such a burst of pride and pathos eight years ago at Lexington and Concord, round out their course with an event less famous, but hardly less worthy of public remembrance. The old New-Yorker of two and three generations ago used to revive it as the "ever-memorable 25th of November, 1783," when the British evacuated the city and left America to her new destiny. If the modern New-Yorker shows a fainter appreciation of it, and smiles, perhaps, at the inadequate procession which annually attempts to keep its memory popular, he nevertheless unconsciously adds to its significance. New York expresses her obligations to that event by what she is. The evacuation of the city by the British meant her escape from colonial thralldom, her commercial as well as political emancipation; and her present greatness is her own best tribute to the importance of the day. While the cosmopolitan character of our population is bound to work a levelling effect, and will tend to repress what should otherwise

Vol. LXVII.—No. 402.—57

Howard Pyle, a famous American illustrator, imagines the sight of the last boat of English troops leaving New York City. This was published in 1883 during the celebration of the 100th anniversary of the end of the war.

Part of the text on this page sums up the importance of this moment: "The evacuation of the city by the British meant her escape from colonial thralldom [servitude], her commercial as well as political emancipation; and her present greatness is her own best tribute to the importance of the day."

CHAPTER 40

... *and a Reckoning*

Woodhull continued to send the occasional report from Long Island, though there was nothing of great urgency or importance anymore. The Culpers had done their duty, and done it well. A note dated July 5, 1783, was accompanied by a final balance record that Woodhull submitted to Tallmadge, at the major's request: "I only kept the most simple account that I possibly could, for fear it should betray me, but I trust it is a just one—and I do assure you I have been as frugal as [I] possibly could. I desire you would explain to the Genl. the circumstances that attended this lengthy correspondence that he may be satisfied that we have not been extravagant." Woodhull then concluded the letter in a way that clearly reflected the present optimistic mood on Long Island: "Wishing you health and happiness, I am your very humble servant, Saml. Culper."

After five years, four major plots thwarted, countless misgivings and close calls, and untold sleepless nights, the Culper correspondence came to an end. The ring had operated effectively from the very heart of the enemy's headquarters and had never been successfully infiltrated, uncovered, or unmasked, despite numerous efforts in that vein. The loss of Agent 355 was a tragedy, but it was also remarkable that the casualties were not much higher, given how close the Culpers were to the enemy in Manhattan and the daring

This 1784 map shows the boundaries of eight of the original thirteen states. Drawn by Lewis Evans, it was published in England in an atlas by Bowles Publishers. In addition to the new states, the map also describes the Native American tribes in the area and their hunting grounds.

maneuvers of the agents on Long Island. While the spies had not been able to deliver Manhattan to Washington before the war's end, they had been his eyes and ears there, enabling him to beat the British even without holding the city. The Culper Ring was a success.

All that remained now between Washington and his spies was the settling of some small monetary debts; the larger debts—the intangible kind, for helping to protect a fledgling nation—could never be fully repaid, nor did the remaining members of the Culper Ring seek out such payment. A return to an open, honest, and simple life, in an independent nation, would be reward enough. And so they hoped, and prayed, and waited for the British to depart from New York at long last, even as the aftermath of war swirled around them.

Afterword

Retaking New York

The British delegation finally signed the Treaty of Paris on September 3, 1783, and Washington's troops were at the ready to ride into Manhattan as the last redcoat left the city. Colonel Tallmadge, however, was concerned for the safety of his spies who had lived and worked as Loyalists during the occupation, knowing they might now find themselves threatened by their newly empowered Patriot neighbors who had no inkling of their true sentiments and bravery. How could Townsend erase the fact that he had run a store that served British soldiers, worked for a Loyalist newspaper, frequented the coffeehouse popular among the officers, and kept company with those who had penetrated the inner circles of the top brass in the city?

From the view of someone on the outside, Robert Townsend had not only enjoyed a rather cushy life during the war but also profited from it. This would hardly sit well with those who had suffered the loss of life, limb, and property for the sake of American independence, and Colonel Tallmadge was fearful that some vengeful Patriot might come looking for his pound of flesh. He was desperate to seek out his spies and contract bodyguards to ensure their personal welfare, send them underground, create for them yet another false identity elsewhere in the city, or even spirit them out of New York for a time until passions cooled.

Tallmadge received permission from General Washington to go into Manhattan to meet with his spies. By all accounts, he was able to meet quietly and safely with Townsend and the others to ensure their security when the British finally evacuated the city. "While at New York I saw and secured all who had been friendly to us through the war, and especially our emissaries," he wrote.

At noon on Tuesday, November 25, 1783—coincidentally, Robert Townsend's thirtieth birthday—Washington rode into Manhattan, with Benjamin Tallmadge among the officers at his side. A contingent rode ahead, scanning the streets as the last of the British officers boarded their ships; Washington followed with his officers and troops spanning eight across. In the previous days and hours leading up to that moment, some joyful Patriots had hoisted American flags over their homes only to have them torn down; in a few cases, they came to blows with redcoat enforcers. But now the citizens of New York, no longer subject to British law or British soldiers, waved flags freely as Washington rode forward. Church bells tolled not in warning but in celebration, and the shouts after each firing of the cannons were triumphant rather than terrified. Some people even crowded the water's edge, waving at the ships set for departure and laughingly bidding the defeated soldiers on board a lovely trip home.

Chapin.
P. Greatbach.
ENTRANCE OF THE AMERICAN ARMY INTO NEW YORK, NOV. 25TH 1783.

A victorious George Washington returns to Manhattan in 1783. Six years later he would be president of the United States and his first seat of government would be in New York City.

Washington's Trip to Long Island: He Never Knew Their Names

In 1790, Washington, now a civilian, made a tour of Long Island to meet the people and examine the damage done to land and property during the British occupation. But he also had it in mind to privately visit with and thank the individuals who had risked so much to gather intelligence and smuggle it to him.

He approached Setauket on April 22 and made a stop at "the House of a Capt. Roe, which is tolerably dect. with obliging people in it." Whether those obliging people with whom he passed several pleasant hours included the rest of the Setauket Culpers—Benjamin Tallmadge, Abraham Woodhull, and Caleb Brewster—or whether he was even aware that he was lodging under the roof of one of those very spies he had journeyed to thank, Washington did not say. His knowledge of the ring members' true identities was, after all, purposely quite limited. He had not wanted to know more than he needed to, in order to protect them, and several of the members (Townsend in particular) had been insistent that Washington never learn their names. The following day he took his leave of Roe's tavern and continued eastward, where his tour took him to Oyster Bay. His brief notes make no mention of a meeting with Robert Townsend or any member of his family, despite Samuel Townsend's numerous run-ins with the law and his suffering as Colonel Simcoe's reluctant landlord. Had Washington been aware of the debt of gratitude that he owed to a certain native son of this town, his stay surely would not have been so brief. Instead, he made his visit, paid his respects to the brave citizens of the town, and rode on, having never met the man he so earnestly sought to thank.

By the time the president crossed the ferry back to Manhattan at sundown on April 24, he had completed his circuit around the part of the island wherein lived the ring of spies who had served him so faithfully and carried out their weighty task with dedication and courage. He had sincerely hoped to have some time with the mysterious Culper Junior, who had risked his life, health, and well-being for so long, passing in and out of the lion's mouth every day, seeking to still the monarch's roar within American borders. But no matter the greetings sent the general's way or the invitations extended, Townsend never stepped out of the shadows to meet with his commander in chief. It would have been a great honor, to be sure, but it was not one that Townsend sought. He did not want praise or celebration; the greatest reward Washington could give him was simply a return to a quiet and unassuming life, as a man subject now to no king but God.

Those few who knew the Culpers' secret kept it close, and all Washington could do was carry gratitude in his heart for the sacrifices of his brave spies, which were no less meaningful for having been made in city streets and country back roads rather than on a battlefield. These men and women had given their all to, as the Preamble to the United States Constitution states, "establish Justice, insure domestic Tranquility, provide for the common defence, promote the general Welfare, and secure the Blessings of Liberty to ourselves and our Posterity."

Appendixes

Postwar Lives of the Culper Ring

CALEB BREWSTER, after his years of excitement rowing back and forth across Long Island Sound in his whaleboat and engaging in hard-fought skirmishes, found that the second part of his life was much quieter than the first, though he was never far from the sea. He married Anne Lewis of Fairfield, Connecticut, in 1784, and moved to a farm at Black Rock, southwest of Bridgeport, Connecticut, where the couple had several children. Brewster passed away at his farm on February 13, 1827, at the age of seventy-nine. For all of his prodigious feats of bravery and skill during the war, his headstone notes his eventual rank of captain and then sums up his service simply: "He was a brave and active officer of the Revolution."

JAMES RIVINGTON had a less tranquil retirement. Rivington and his shop received special protection in the days and weeks following the British evacuation from New York City; there would be no burning and looting, as had occurred at the hands of the Sons of Liberty in 1775. He remained in New York, though his newspaper business suffered because of his reputation as a staunch enemy of the new republic. He was eventually forced to close his shop, and with eight children to support back in England, several bad investments, and a personal taste for the high life, his financial situation deteriorated until he served time in debtors' prison. He died in New York, where he had spent thirty-six of his seventy-eight years of life, on July 4, 1802.

AUSTIN ROE, like Caleb Brewster, achieved the rank of captain, and carried that title proudly for the rest of his life. He and his wife, the former Catherine Jones, had eight children. In 1798, the family moved from Setauket on the northern shore of Long Island to Patchogue, almost exactly opposite on the southern shore, and opened a hotel. Unlike many of the other Culpers, Roe enjoyed sharing stories of his spying adventures with locals and patrons at his inn, though he was careful to protect the privacy of his fellow ring members. He passed away on November 29, 1830, at the age of eighty-one.

BENJAMIN TALLMADGE married Mary Floyd, daughter of Major General William Floyd, a signer of the Declaration of Independence. The couple moved to Connecticut, where they had seven children. In 1792, Tallmadge was appointed postmaster for the town of Litchfield. He would later serve sixteen years in the House of Representatives (1801–17). Tallmadge died on March 7, 1835. He was eighty-one years old.

ROBERT TOWNSEND never spoke of his service, never applied for a pension, never corrected those who assumed he had done nothing but tend his shop during the war, and never, it seems, recovered emotionally from the blow of Agent 355's capture and imprisonment. After the war he grew even more reserved and reclusive, staying near his brothers and their families but never marrying himself. Townsend developed strong abolitionist beliefs and staunchly opposed any type of slave ownership; later in life he worked on behalf of some former slaves of his father's to help them gain their freedom. The man once known as Culper Junior died exactly three years after Benjamin Tallmadge, on March 7, 1838, at the age of eighty-four.

ABRAHAM WOODHULL married Mary Smith in 1781. He lived in Setauket for the rest of his life, where he raised three children and served in various senior positions in the Suffolk County government. He never spoke much about his role in the spy ring. He passed away on January 23, 1826, at the age of seventy-six, and was buried in the Setauket Presbyterian Church graveyard. In 1936, the Mayflower Chapter of the Daughters of the American Revolution erected the following marker near his simple headstone:

> Friend and confidant of George Washington, Head of Long Island Secret Service during the Revolution, and operated under the alias of Samuel Culper, Sr. To him and his associates have been credited a large share in the success of the army of the Revolution. Born in Setauket Oct. 7, 1750 in the original Woodhull homestead, Son of Richard Woodhull and Margaret Smith. Fifth generation from Richard Woodhull, the original grantee of a large portion of Brookhaven Town. He was a Presbyterian occupying a "Pew of Authority" in the old church, and doing much toward the building of the new church. Was a man of integrity punctual and precise in

his business relations. He freed his slaves long before they were legally free. Filled numerous important positions being magistrate in Setauket many years, Judge of the Court of Common Pleas 1793 to 1799, first Judge of Suffolk Co. from 1799 to 1810.

AGENT 355, whose name and fate have both been lost to time, might have escaped imprisonment and gone on to live a long and happy life. Or she might have passed away somewhere in the dark, disease-infested hull of HMS *Jersey*. When the British left New York in November 1783, they abandoned the *Jersey* in the harbor, with several thousand starving prisoners still on board.

Washington's Time as a Spy

Two decades earlier, in 1754, the British army (consisting of both soldiers from the motherland and local colonial militias) had launched a war in North America against the French army and native tribes who were attacking British citizens in regions granted in previous treaties to the British government. For the next nine years, the continent was embroiled in battles to control the various outposts and forts sprinkled across the wilderness regions of the Ohio River and Appalachian Mountains.

The previous year, Washington, just twenty-one years old, volunteered to engage with the French soldiers and learn whatever he could about their intentions and fortifications through leading conversations, as well as whatever was carelessly shared over wine bottles. As it did throughout his life, Washington's temperate nature served him well on that mission, as he maintained his sobriety and clearheadedness so that he could report back to his superiors that the French had no intentions of quitting the country without a fight.

The Significance of the Culper Ring

As set up by Washington and Tallmadge, the Culper Ring had several advantages over other spy rings, and its success helped shape intelligence operations for years to come.

First, they had an added layer of security: not every member was aware of the identities of the others in the ring.

Second, the Culpers had developed a complex network that allowed Woodhull, Brewster, or Roe to add intelligence en route to General Washington, confirming or correcting the initial reports, so the information was more detailed when it finally reached its intended destination.

Third, the Culpers were able to operate in a wide social circle because the members were citizens from all walks of life. Townsend gathered information from soldiers around the city and sailors at the dock; Agent 355 charmed strategic details out of high-ranking officers at parties; Rivington repeated gossip and plans overheard in his shop; Woodhull enhanced these reports with his own observations of troop activities on Long Island and recounted what shop owners were saying or if there was an uptick in lumber sales or ship repairs; Roe learned whatever news was shared when tongues loosened in his tavern; and from the water Brewster spied on British naval movements.

Communicate in Secret

USE INVISIBLE INK

Invisible ink was widely used in Europe and the colonies in the 1700s. George Washington knew this and asked a chemist friend to take the technique one step further. He asked for an ink that could only be made visible using a secret stain. Then the ink and the precious stain were delivered to his spies.

Washington's spies wrote messages in invisible ink between the lines of ordinary letters, reports, or store inventory lists. If captured, the papers would not raise any suspicions.

When the spies were being especially careful, they wrote a message on a blank sheet of paper and slipped the sheet into a pile of blank paper. But they had to let the receiver know which sheet of paper had the message on it. Sometimes they folded a corner, but that could easily be detected. So they made a tiny mark or dot on the sheet with the message, sometimes on the back so it was hard to notice at a quick glance.

You can communicate using invisible ink, too. You can write messages on paper that will seem blank, or write your messages between the lines of sentences written in pencil or pen.

Lemon juice, milk, and onion juice make good ink. (Milk and lemon juice are easy. Onion juice is smelly and harder to make.)

For lemon juice ink, cut a lemon in half and squeeze the juice into a bowl. For milk ink, simply pour milk into a bowl. Onion ink is made with a three-step process: cut the onion in half, grate some of it carefully into a bowl, and let it stand until you see liquid gathering in the bottom of the bowl.

Write your message on the thickest white paper you can find.

Your writing instrument can be the end of a chopstick, a toothpick, or a cotton swab. Think of your message in advance, because it's sometimes hard to see where you have already written a word. Make sure you let your invisible ink dry completely.

Now, let's see if you can expose what you've written.

- For lemon juice and onion juice messages, pass the paper carefully over the top of a toaster that has just popped up. Be sure to wear oven mitts while doing this.

- For milk messages, you'll need to rub graphite over the paper. The lead in pencils is graphite. You can get some from a pencil sharpener drawer, or you can ask an adult to scrape some off of a pencil. Rub the graphite very gently over the paper and your message will appear!

USE AN ALPHABETICAL CODE

The first code that Benjamin Tallmadge set up is called an alphabetical code. He opened a dictionary to the first page and started to make a list of all the words he thought would be important in gathering information about British actions—words such as "artillery," "lumber," "ships," "supplies," and "troops." The dictionary helped him think of all the possible words. He wrote them in alphabetical order and then assigned each one a unique number, starting with the number 1. Then he added people's names and places to the list. In the end, there were 763 words in his code, each with a unique number.

This kind of code is usually used by inexperienced spies, because it is easy to decode. If the enemy figures out that a message is in this kind of code, they could figure out that numbers close together might start with the same letter. They might also know that smaller numbers—in the twenties and thirties, for example—would represent words at the beginning of the alphabet (the code for "attack" was 38) and that larger numbers, such as 700, would begin with letters at the end of the alphabet (the code for "wagon" was 703).

There are many other ways to make up codes and send messages. These three books have lots of ideas:

Blackwood, Gary. *Mysterious Messages: A History of Codes and Ciphers*. New York: Scholastic, 2009.

Janeczko, Paul B. *Top Secret: A Handbook of Codes, Ciphers, and Secret Writing*. Cambridge, Mass.: Candlewick Press, 2004.

O'Brien, Eileen, and Diana Riddell. *The Usborne Book of Secret Codes*. London: Usborne Publishing, 1997.

I

- s 280
- f 281
- in 282
- is 283
- it 284
- ice 285
- ink 286
- into 287
- instance 288
- island 289
- impress 290
- impression 291
- incamp 292
- incur 293
- infest 294
- inforce 295
- instance 296
- inmans 297
- instruct 298
- intrigue 299
- interest 300
- instant 301
- invest 302
- invite 303
- ignorant 304
- imprudent 305
- industry 306
- infamous 307
- influence 308
- infantry 309
- infantry 310
- injury 311
- [illegible] 312
- instrument 313
- intimate 314
- illegal 315
- imagin 316
- important 317
- imprison 318
- improper 319
- incumber 320
- inhuman 321
- inquiry 322
- interview 323
- inward 324
- intercede 325
- interfere 326
- intermix 327
- introduce 328
- immediate 329
- impertinent 330
- incouragement 331
- infection 332
- irregular 333
- inlead 334
- indians 335

J

- June 336
- July 337
- jury 338
- jealous 339
- justify 340
- January 341

K

- key 342
- king 343
- kill 344
- know 345

L

- law 346
- land 347
- love 348
- low 349
- lot 350
- lord 351
- light 352
- last 353
- learn 354
- lady 355
- letter 356
- levy 357
- lover now 358
- liar 359
- lucky 360
- language 361
- limit 362
- liquid 363
- longitude 364
- latitude 365
- laudable 366
- legible 367
- liberty 368
- lottery 369
- literature 370

M

- man 371
- map 372
- may 373
- march 374
- mast 375
- make 376
- met 377
- me 378
- my 379
- much 380
- move 381

M

- most 382
- mind 383
- many 384
- mercy 385
- moment 386
- murder 387
- measure 388
- method 389
- mischief 390
- mistake 391
- molest 392
- majesty 393
- meditate 394
- memory 395
- messenger 396
- misery 397
- moveable 398
- multitude 399
- miscarry 400
- misfortune 401
- miserable 402
- mercenary 403
- majority 404
- minority 405
- memorial 406
- misterious 407
- manufacture 408
- moderator 409
- ministerial 410

N

- name 411
- new 412
- no 413
- not 414
- night 415
- never 416
- needful 417
- number 418
- neither 419
- nothing 420
- neglect 421
- nation 422
- navy 423
- natural 424
- negative 425
- negligence 426
- novemb. 427
- necessary 428
- nobility 429

O

- oath 430
- of 431
- off 432

30742 O

- on 433
- or 434
- out 435
- offer 436
- office 437
- owe 438
- order 439
- over 440
- obstruct 441
- obtain 442
- observe 443
- occur 444
- offence 445
- omit 446
- oppose 447
- obligate 448
- obstinate 449
- obviate 450
- occupy 451
- operate 452
- origin 453
- ornament 454
- overcome 455
- overlook 456
- overtake 457
- owner 458
- overthrow 459
- obedience 460
- objection 461
- october 462
- obscure 463
- occasion 464
- opinion 465
- oppression 466
- opportunity 467
- obligation 468

P

- pay 469
- peace 470
- plan 471
- put 472
- port 473
- proof 474
- please 475
- part 476
- paper 477
- pardon 478
- party 479
- perfect 480

A page from one of the code books the ring put together shows how they replaced names and places with numbers.

Timeline

1765

MARCH 22

England passes the Stamp Act, levying a tax on every piece of paper the colonists use: newspapers, legal documents, bills, and even playing cards.

AUGUST

The colonists secretly found the Sons of Liberty to organize protests against the Stamp Act.

1768

OCTOBER

British troops land in Boston to squash the rebellious colonists.

1770

MARCH 5

A clash between Patriots and British soldiers in Boston becomes known as the Boston Massacre.

1773

SPRING

James Rivington establishes his print shop in lower Manhattan and begins publishing his first newspaper.

DECEMBER 16

The Sons of Liberty dump tea from merchant ships into Boston Harbor to protest thirteen years of increasing oppression.

1774

JANUARY 16

Abraham Woodhull inherits his family's homestead in Setauket, New York.

JUNE 2

The British pass the Quartering Act of 1774, which requires colonists to provide rooms and meals to British soldiers.

SEPTEMBER 5

The First Continental Congress meets in Philadelphia with representatives from the colonies.

1775

APRIL 19

The Patriots and the British fight at Lexington and Concord, firing "the shot heard round the world."

The Siege of Boston begins.

MAY 10

The Second Continental Congress meets in Philadelphia.

JUNE 15
George Washington is named commander of the Continental Army.

JUNE 17
The Patriots and the British fight at the Battle of Bunker Hill.

1776

MARCH 17
The Siege of Boston ends with a victory for the Patriots.

JUNE 20
Benjamin Tallmadge joins the Continental Army in Connecticut.

JULY 3
The British begin the invasion of New York City.

JULY 4
The Declaration of Independence is adopted.

AUGUST 27
The Battle of Long Island.

SEPTEMBER 22
Nathan Hale is hanged as a spy.

DECEMBER 25-26
Washington and his army cross the Delaware River and capture Trenton, New Jersey.

1777

DECEMBER 19
General Washington establishes his winter camp in Valley Forge, Pennsylvania.

1778

FEBRUARY 6

France agrees to provide supplies and troops to fight alongside the Patriots.

JUNE 18

The British abandon Philadelphia and move troops to New York.

LATE SUMMER

Benjamin Tallmadge recruits the first members of the Culper spy ring.

AUGUST 29

The Battle of Rhode Island.

NOVEMBER 23

Abraham Woodhull writes his first letter to General Washington.

1779

MAY

Benedict Arnold first contacts British General Clinton.

SUMMER

Robert Townsend joins the ring.

SEPTEMBER (?)

The mysterious Agent 355 is recruited.

NOVEMBER 27

The ring exposes the British counterfeiting plot.
Rivington throws in his lot with the Patriots.

1780

JULY 11

French troops land in Rhode Island.

SEPTEMBER 25

Information gathered by the ring exposes Benedict Arnold as a traitor.

OCTOBER 2

John André is hanged.

1782

FEBRUARY 27

The British House of Commons votes to end all offensive actions against the colonists.

1783

SEPTEMBER 3

The British government formally acknowledges the United States of America. Thousands of Loyalists leave to settle in Canada or England.

NOVEMBER 25

Washington rides into Manhattan as the victor as the last British ships leave the harbor.

~

Selected Sources

Allen, Thomas B., and Cheryl Harness. *George Washington, Spymaster: How America Outspied the British and Won the Revolutionary War.* Washington D.C.: National Geographic, 2004.
A highly accessible book, this is a great starting point for adults and older children alike who are interested in the spying activities under Washington's command during the Revolution. It is the result of solid research and offers a good overview of espionage activities throughout the war.

Bakeless, John Edwin. *Turncoats, Traitors, and Heroes.* New York: Da Capo, 1998.
This work provides a look at the unfortunate incident of Nathan Hale, the saga of Benedict Arnold's treachery, and many other covert operations in the American theater during the war, including the incredible adventure of John Champe and his attempt to kidnap Arnold back for the Patriots.

Baker, William S. "Itinerary of General Washington from June 15, 1775, to December 23, 1783." *The Pennsylvania Magazine of History and Biography* 15, no. 1 (1891): 41–87. http://jstor.org.

Crary, Catherine Snell. "The Tory and the Spy: The Double Life of James Rivington," *The William and Mary Quarterly,* 3rd ser., 16, no. 1 (January 1959): 61–72. Accessed online March 22, 2013.
This article pulls together a number of primary sources that shed light on Rivington's spying activities, including his contribution to the victory at Yorktown, that were previously discounted as apocryphal, and therefore unreliable, by many historians.

Fernow, Brian, ed. *Documents Relating to the Colonial History of the State of New York*. Vol. 15. State Archives, vol. 1. Albany, NY: Weed, Parsons and Company, 1887.

"George Washington and the Culper Spy Ring." Stony Brook University Libraries. http://guides.library.stonybrook.edu/culper-spy-ring.

Kerber, Linda K. *Women of the Republic: Intellect and Ideology in Revolutionary America*. Chapel Hill: University of North Carolina Press, 1997.

Macy, Harry, Jr. "Robert Townsend, Jr., of New York City." *The New York Genealogical and Biographical Record* 126 (1995): 25–34, 108–12, 192–98.
Perhaps more than any other single source, this article shed light on the physical appearance and relationships of the Townsend family and also offered an in-depth look at Robert Townsend and his interaction with the child named Robert Townsend Jr. after the war.

Nagy, John A. *Invisible Ink: Spycraft of the American Revolution*. Yardley, PA: Westholme, 2010.
Nagy has compiled a searching and fascinating examination of various techniques used by spies throughout the American colonies and abroad to communicate covertly. His exploration of the history of invisible ink prior to the Culper stain's development by Sir James Jay, as well as the use of that particular formula, was tremendously helpful for this book.

———. *Spies in the Continental Capital: Espionage Across Pennsylvania During the American Revolution*. Yardley, PA: Westholme, 2011.

New York Gazette & Weekly. Templeton & Stewart. April 25, 1774. Mercury issue 1174, p. 2.

———. Templeton & Stewart. August 15, 1774. Mercury issue 1192, p. 4.

———. Templeton & Stewart. February 27, 1775. Mercury issue 1220, p. 3.

Norton, Mary Beth. *Liberty's Daughters: The Revolutionary Experience of American Women, 1750–1800*. Ithaca, NY: Cornell University Press, 1996.
A fascinating compilation of primary sources, this book offers valuable insight into the challenges and perils of women living in war-torn areas during the Revolution, including the letter from Lord Rawdon about the outbreak of sexual assaults against ladies in British-occupied Staten Island.

Paul, Joel Richard. *Unlikely Allies: How a Merchant, a Playwright, and a Spy Saved the American Revolution*. New York: Riverhead, 2009.
A detailed account of the covert activities of the French government via the fabricated Roderigue Hortalez & Company, Paul's research offers a dynamic and intriguing reconstruction of the events leading up to, and resulting from, the smuggling efforts.

Pennypacker, Morton. *General Washington's Spies*. Walnut Creek, CA: Aegean Park, 1999.
Pennypacker's 1939 publication of the Culper letters includes a narrative of many of the events involving the ring, as they were known at the time, as well as both transcripts and photographs of many of the original letters exchanged between several of the ring's members, Tallmadge, and Washington. It was absolutely invaluable not only to the composition of this book but also to understanding the Culper story in general.

———. *Two Spies: Nathan Hale and Robert Townsend*. Boston and New York: Houghton Mifflin, 1930.

Pierce, Kara. "A Revolutionary Masquerade: The Chronicles of James Rivington." Binghamton University. n.d. http://wwwz.binghampton.edu/history/esources/journal-of-history/chronicles-of-james-rivington.html.
Pierce's article offers a fascinating look into the personal life of James Rivington as well as his spying activities during the war and was an important resource in helping to reconstruct Rivington's mysterious character.

Pierce, Susan M. *The History of Raynham Hall*. Thesis, Columbia University, 1986.
This thesis study provided many helpful details about the architectural history of the Townsend family homestead and its position in colonial Oyster Bay.

Rose, Alexander. *Washington's Spies: The Story of America's First Spy Ring*. New York: Bantam, 2006.
Rose undertook a tremendous depth of research to complete his book, and it served as an excellent starting point in quite a few places for our own investigation into the matter. Especially helpful was his engagement with disparate primary sources that together formed a fuller picture of the Culper Ring's activities and accomplishments.

Ross, Peter. "A Few Revolutionary Heroes—General Woodhull—Colonel Tallmadge—General Parsons—Colonel Meigs." *A History of Long Island, from Its Earliest Settlement to the Present Time*. New York and Chicago: Lewis, 1902.

Schecter, Barnet. *The Battle for New York: The City at the Heart of the American Revolution*. New York: Walker, 2002.
This book proved especially important in helping us to understand the vital importance of New York City to the overall outcome of the war and allowed us to better grasp the significance of its political, strategic, and symbolic impact. It also helped us explain the high regard that Washington had for his spy network within the city.

Tallmadge, Benjamin. *Memoir of Colonel Benjamin Tallmadge Prepared by Himself at the Request of His Children*. New York: Thomas Holman, 1858. Reprint, New York: *New York Times*, 1968.
Most of the accounts of Tallmadge's activities and emotions come directly from his own pen in the memoirs he originally wrote in the final years of his life and first published for widespread distribution in 1858. Rarely is an author so lucky as to have the impressions and reflections of a historical figure in his original words. This is an especially valuable resource for any student of the American Revolution or Washington's spycraft.

Townsend, Robert. "Account Book of Robert Townsend, Merchant, of Oyster Bay Township, N.Y., and New York, N.Y., Begun November 23, 1779, and Continued to March 29, 1781." Transcription. East Hampton Library, Long Island Collection, East Hampton, NY.
The firsthand information revealed in this document was extremely helpful in understanding more about how Townsend operated first in Oyster Bay and later in Manhattan. Both the detailed entries and the periods of inactivity reveal a great deal about Townsend's patterns of behavior, possible emotional struggles, and business habits in managing his shop and his daily life.

Woodhull, Mary Gould, and Francis Bowes Stevens. *Woodhull Genealogy: The Woodhull Family in England and America*. Philadelphia: H. T. Coates, 1904.

Photo credits: pp. 2, 4, 5, 11, 33, 36, 38, 39, 76, 93, 95, 98, 106, 111, 124, 126: Library of Congress Prints and Photographs Division; pp. 74 and 147: Library of Congress Manuscript Division; pp. 14, 16, 19, 21, 40, 47, 63, 66, 105, 109, 129: Art and Picture Collection, The New York Public Library; pp. 82 and 83: Manuscripts and Archives Division, New York Public Library; pp. 12, 15, 28, 41, 64, 73 (top), 99, 113: The Miriam and Ira D. Wallach Division of Art, Prints and Photographs: Print Collection, The New York Public Library; pp. 17, 52, 131: Lionel Pincus and Princess Friyal Map Division, The New York Public Library; pp. 43: Used by permission, Collection of the Litchfield Historical Society; pp. 54: Courtesy of Kurt Knapp Photography; pp. 62: Used by permission, The Friends of Raynham Hall, Inc.; pp. 72, 73 (bottom), 112, 135: Used by permission, Collection of New-York Historical Society

Cover image: Museum of Fine Arts, Boston, William Francis Warden Fund, John H. and Ernestine A. Payne Fund, Commonwealth Cultural Preservation Trust. Jointly owned by the Museum of Fine Arts, Boston, and the National Portrait Gallery, Washington D.C. 1980.1

Index